Teaching Entrepreneurship to Undergraduates

Teaching Entrepreneurship to Undergraduates

Colin Jones

University of Tasmania, Australia

Edward Elgar
Cheltenham, UK • Northampton, MA, USA

Published by
Edward Elgar Publishing Limited
The Lypiatts
15 Lansdown Road
Cheltenham
Glos GL50 2JA
UK

Edward Elgar Publishing, Inc.
William Pratt House
9 Dewey Court
Northampton
Massachusetts 01060
USA

A catalogue record for this book
is available from the British Library

Library of Congress Control Number: 2011924307

ISBN 978 1 84980 406 6

Printed and bound by MPG Books Group, UK

Contents

Figures

Tables

Foreword

I believe this to be the first book in the world to attempt an in-depth exploration of both the philosophy and practice of entrepreneurship education. As such it embodies a number of unique (and entrepreneurial) characteristics. Its emphasis is not upon teaching but on processes of learning. It is written by an entrepreneur who has experience of failure and builds upon a personal learning journey from entrepreneur to teacher and therefore has many thought-provoking insights. The main focus is upon the needs of student learners in higher education and the importance of their taking ownership of learning. The text seeks to demonstrate what this means in practice, how to build upon what learners already know and what they can bring to the party from very diverse perspectives. Unlike many other books in this field it is not prescriptive. It presents a debate and is designed to encourage the reader to think, reflect and indeed argue. It places ownership with, and challenges the reader with a style of personal dialogue.

The book will help entrepreneurship educators defend their approach outside of the conventional home of the business school. It will also help in defence of the place of entrepreneurship education in wider educational philosophy. But it does not eschew dealing with some of the 'conventions' of business education, for example the business plan, ideas generation and their realisation in practice and most interestingly the development of the personal capacity to 'sell' as opposed to the broader approaches to 'market planning'.

Although a very strong personal philosophy guides the text there is no hesitation in exploring the wider world of entrepreneurship education internationally and the variety of views and approaches therein. Most importantly for me it emphasises importance of the personal development of the individual, the value in using the reflections and views of the learner (of which there are many examples) and of taking a stance on what are the important entrepreneurial attributes that the facilitator should seek to enhance via the process of learning. Not all will agree with the choices made but one suspects that the author knows this and sees the proposals he makes as part of a thought-provoking process. Every dedicated entrepreneurship educator will benefit from this book.

Allan Gibb
Professor Emeritus, University of Durham, UK

Acknowledgements

I am eternally grateful to the students I have encountered in my various classes at the University of Tasmania. Without their trust and sense of adventure, this book would not have been possible. They have continually served as the source of my inspiration to explore the field of entrepreneurship education. More often than not I have been their student.

During my journey so far I have met many incredible educators who have shared many wonderful ideas with me and given me the motivation to further develop my own ideas. In a sense many of the ideas presented here have been co-authored by my current and past students and the many educators I have conversed with. To you all I sincerely say thank you. A special thanks to Dr Polly McGee for her valuable feedback on my earlier drafts.

Two colleagues in particular have greatly assisted my scholarly progress thus far. The first is Associate Professor Jack English, who took a chance recruiting me into academia without much more than a hunch to be guided by. The second is Professor Harry Matlay, who has supported the publication of my thoughts and ideas since the first time we met. We cannot travel far without the guidance and care of suitable mentors, and in that regard, I have been extremely fortunate.

This book is dedicated to several people. Firstly it is dedicated to my father David, who has always inspired me to believe that the things we dream of can indeed be created. Secondly, it is dedicated to Maureen Williamson, a wonderful educator who convinced me that we are all entitled to dream. Thirdly, this book is dedicated to all of my past, current and future students and to my entrepreneurship education colleagues scattered around the globe who also dare to dream. Lastly, it is dedicated to Kathryn, Natasha, Delsen and Turlican, who all endure my frequent time away from home as I attempt to explore and understand the global landscape of entrepreneurship education.

Introduction

Let us be clear as to the aim of this text: it is not the intention to suggest *what* should be taught, or *how* to teach entrepreneurship (or enterprise) to undergraduates, hereinafter referred to as EE. Rather, the aim of this text is to provoke deeper engagement with *how to think about teaching EE* in higher education. Thus, the focus is not so much on how to teach, but rather upon how students learn. Indeed, this text is developed unashamedly from a learner-centred perspective. It will be my own personal experiences and observations of EE in higher education, along with the views of other EE educators, that set the parameters for the direction of the text. Stated another way, this text does not aim to connect to, or extend the ideas found in mainstream popular texts. In contrast, this text aims to challenge every individual EE educator to 1) develop their own 'student specific' learning outcomes, 2) conceive a variety of learning activities through which their identified learning outcomes can be achieved, and 3) construct appropriate (and authentic) assessment processes to guide the development of students' learning; and to do so having thoughtfully considered the various issues introduced and discussed throughout the following chapters. Let us first consider the purpose of each chapter.

CHAPTER SUMMARIES

Chapter 1   Your Teaching Philosophy

The first chapter is premised upon a fundamental question: how do students learn to *be* entrepreneurial? Answering this important question has been the driving force behind the development of a unique approach to EE at the University of Tasmania (UTAS). It has led to the development of a unique teaching philosophy that has underpinned the development of a truly learner-centred EE programme, previously referred to as the *hic et nunc* model.[1] This chapter aims to allow the reader to 1) locate themselves to the approaches discussed here vis-à-vis their own approach and teaching philosophy, and 2) provide a simple working example of how EE programmes can evolve over time. This chapter is deliberately reflective and aims to calm the reader by elevating the needs of the student above those of the educator, school or institution. Recognising the centrality of the various dialogic relationships that exist in higher education (i.e. the outcomes of students, educators, schools and institutions cannot be fully explained without reference to at least one of the other elements) allows the reader to reconceptualise the environments they operate in. Finally, the controversial notion that at least half of what the student needs to learn already resides inside the student. That it is the task of the educator to expose the student to situations from which they can (via deep self and group reflection) challenge various epistemological assumptions that in turn open up new learning pathways. In summary, Chapter 1 exposes the reader to the author's teaching philosophy and challenges the reader to create/account for their own teaching philosophy.

Chapter 2 Entrepreneurship Education

Chapter 2 moves away from the author's underlying philosophy to consider briefly the history of EE, current approaches and debates within higher education. Attention is drawn to more than 44 identified teaching pedagogies for EE in higher education[2] to highlight the challenges and opportunities that arise from revisiting the issue of how EE is commonly taught in higher education. This chapter also serves to introduce a number of educators from across the globe whose ideas and thoughts are woven into the discussion throughout this book. This chapter therefore allows the reader to become familiar with contemporary debates in the global delivery of EE. Debates that can be contrasted against the author's personal perspective as to the challenges confronting educators in this domain.

Chapter 3 The Ontological Dilemma

This rather ambitious chapter commences with a focus upon a raft of concerns that have started to emerge related to the societal value of EE,[3] the primary elements of EE,[4] and the overall legitimacy of EE in higher education.[5] Within this chapter, an argument based on consideration of the ontology of EE is presented. The key issue is the development of an explanation of *how* and *when* students become entrepreneurial. Whereas medical students graduate as doctors, engineering students as engineers and education students as educators, students of entrepreneurship/enterprise rarely graduate as entrepreneurs (in the business start-up sense). Clearly, it is important to determine what knowledge and/or other forms of realisable value are actually gained from EE that can be used upon graduation. It is also important to understand why graduates of EE face unique challenges in the quest to acquire specific knowledge and/or specific skills prior to graduation.

A process of continuous reflection is argued to support the development of entrepreneurial capacity via the modification of each student's habits of thought. To contextualise this issue, the opinions of other educators regarding what are the primary forms of value derived from EE are also presented. The chapter concludes with a series of challenges that the educator might consider to ensure the inherent ontological challenges of EE are tackled in the development of appropriate curricula.

Chapter 4   The Reasonable Adventurer

Chapter 4 provides an example of how resource profile development is possible through the deliberate crafting of a pro-student development curriculum. Achieved at UTAS through the inclusion of the reasonable adventurer[6] concept, it has required a shift in the curriculum focus to ensure learning activities are designed to support the development of the six attributes of the reasonable adventurer. The first attribute is *intellectectuality*, the ability to alternate between being a believer and a sceptic. The second attribute is *close friendships*, or the ability to discover and understand the individuality of others. The third attribute is *independence in value judgements*, or the ability to rely upon personal experience rather than known external authorities. The fourth attribute is a *tolerance of ambiguity*, or the ability to view life as a series of interruptions and recoveries.[7] The fifth attribute is the *breadth of interest*, or an uncommon interest in the commonplace. The last attribute is a balanced *sense of humour*, or a benign, but lively sense of humour that distinguishes the reasonable adventurer, making him or her good company. So the aim has become focused on creating a fully functioning graduate, one that is capable of using his or her individuality in ways that are beyond their pre-existing mental endowments.

Essentially, the role of the educator has become increasingly refined. Gone is the assumption of future entrepreneurial glory by our graduates. In its place has risen a concern for allowing the students to grow in their here and now.[8] The issue of how other EE educators tackle this student development issue is canvassed to provide the reader with alternative motivations to stimulate imaginative thoughts as to how their own curriculum might also be shaped to free students from themselves. The critical issue to emerge from this chapter: that we as educators must always be challenging ourselves vis-à-vis our role and purpose in the development and delivery of EE.

Chapter 5 Student Diversity

This chapter aims to advance beyond notions of students as individual learners. At the heart of my approach is an aim to exploit student interaction so as to significantly advance student learning outcomes. Acknowledging the overall increasing presence of student diversity within the higher education sector[9] provides educators with a unique opportunity. Building upon past research that highlights the relationship between increased superior learning outcomes from exposure to higher levels of student diversity,[10] the *hic et nunc* model deliberately uses student diversity in a positive way. The first challenge for any educator attempting to harness diversity in the student body is to identify the dimensions of any such diversity. Within this chapter, an index of student similarity is presented to illustrate a simple way of identifying the degree of diversity present within any learning environment. An index that facilitates simple comparisons between students, classes and cohorts. Essentially, the 'elephant in the room' is asked to step forward and contribute, rather than be silent (and hidden) in the corner. Importantly, the students are informed of the nature of the diversity in the room and this recognition forms an important part of their preparation for the reflection exercises.

Finally, the issue of how student diversity is dealt with by other educators is discussed. The aim of this discussion is not merely to balance the author's arguments, but also to excite the reader of the endless possibilities to enlist diversity as a new and valuable addition to the learning environment.

Chapter 6 The Learning Environment

Chapter 6 highlights the potentially important role of the student in shaping the nature of the learning environments within which they interact. It is proposed that the use of constructive alignment in tandem with a learner-centred approach containing criterion-based assessment can empower students in important ways. That such empowerment can go further than increasing their ability to learn to also include an additional role in helping to shape their learning environment. The use of an evolutionary approach within this chapter helps facilitate discussion of the often-neglected process of niche construction through which such possible empowerment is enacted. The primary drivers of the processes discussed are regular summative and formative feedback.

The assertion is that a student's habits of thought are susceptible to change once the student understands how they contribute to their overall fitness vis-à-vis satisfying the stated learning objectives. The implications of the arguments within this chapter go to the very heart of enacting the philosophy of learner-centred approaches to teaching and learning. The opportunity to work with students to achieve both superior learning outcomes and learning environments is highlighted as an important consequence of being truly learner centred. Of critical importance for EE students is the development of confidence,[11] an acknowledged component of why entrepreneurs initiate business start-ups and maintain strong levels of resilience. Again, the key ideas discussed in this chapter are considered against the degree of traction they hold for other EE educators. The aim is to once again create a reflective space for the reader to contemplate how the shifting nature of the learning environment can be used to positively increase the learning outcomes of our students.

Chapter 7   The Resource Profile

The aim of Chapter 7 is to discuss the underlying tools our students must develop/use in order to succeed in their future endeavours. From the perspective of making sense of the entrepreneurial journeys[12] our students may contemplate and indeed attempt, few ideas hold more explanatory power than the notion of a *resource profile*.[13] When we encourage our students to visualise an entrepreneurial business start-up and work towards this outcome, we must be mindful of the social, human and financial capital each student has vis-à-vis that particular idea under consideration. In the absence of the prerequisite resource profile (hereinafter referred to as RP), graduate entrepreneurship (as related to business start-up) is more often than not too challenging.[14]

Within this chapter we will consider two variations of RP thinking, the first related to *RP downsizing* and the second to *RP upsizing*. RP downsizing is the use of small entrepreneurial challenges through which students plan to achieve an outcome and subsequently succeed and/or fail (in varying degrees) followed by reflection as to how their individual/team RP influenced the outcome achieved. RP upsizing is a mapping exercise in which the express *resource* needs (of an individual) for a particular idea are documented, and then collated across the class. Other members of the class help to upsize the RPs of fellow classmates by loaning their contacts, knowledge and access to specific resources to their fellow classmates.

The importance and/or development of the students' RP are also considered from the perspective of what other practices exist in EE globally. Once again, the aim is that through elevating this issue to the reader's attention, a reflection space has been created from within which possible strategies can be conceived as to how to assist the reader's students to understand the importance of RP development.

Chapter 8   The Art of Selling

Chapter 8 unashamedly is intent on refuting the urban (academic) myth that *marketing is not selling*. Entrepreneurial marketing is action-oriented behaviour that combines strategic intent with an individual's capacity to sell ideas and oneself. In the absence of a capacity to sell, the potential value of various forms of strategic knowledge will quite likely dissolve. Put simply, our graduates must walk alone when they begin their entrepreneurial journeys. They cannot rely upon others to advance their cause; initially the responsibility will quite frequently fall on their shoulders.

Entrepreneurial marketing is condensed down to two seemingly simple, but in reality very exacting questions. First, what are you selling to whom?[15] Second, does a compelling reason exist for your customer to buy? To the extent that our students are capable of answering these questions and communicating their justification, they are well on the way to being capable salespersons. The obvious challenge; how to develop such a capacity? This chapter addresses this issue, adding to the author's views alternative ideas from other EE educators. The ultimate aim is to convince the reader of the importance of developing such a capacity. Further, to stimulate the reader's imagination as to how such a capacity might be developed.

Chapter 9   Evaluating Ideas

Chapter 9 is focused upon the evaluation of new ideas. The nascent entrepreneur is frequently inundated with multiple ideas whilst being inexperienced and lacking the required insight to choose between ideas. In this chapter, a structured method for the early assessment of ideas[16] is outlined that is designed to identify new ideas with genuine commercial merit. Many students believe that the leap from a new idea to market entry is only a short distance and they often do not recognise how complex, costly and time consuming the process can be. Consequently, it is important to be able to assess the commercial feasibility of a new idea very early in the innovation process because it is the least costly stage in which to identify and eliminate likely failures.

Just as there are numerous pedagogies associated with teaching EE, determinations of commercial potential abound. In this chapter, various evaluative frameworks are introduced and the proclaimed merits of each are offered for the reader's consideration. The aim being to encourage the reader to ensure that the needs of their students are well served through the provision of a sound and effective means of evaluating ideas.

Chapter 10   Business Plans

The contentious issue of the value of the business plan with higher education is addressed in Chapter 10. Frequently assumed to be a capstone activity in the EE, the business plan has a chequered past. Recently, concern[17] has surfaced that draws into question the underlying value of the business plan as a *must do* learning activity in EE. Within this chapter this important issue is explored and the various sides of the debate considered. An alternative form of business plan is presented for consideration; a plan within which the ontological reality of the student looms large. From this perspective a trilemma is tackled head on, with the student's RP set against an explanation of the conditions under which value can be created and captured and conversely, the conditions under which value cannot be created and/or captured. Within this approach, the traditional business plan headings become meaningless. They are superseded by a narrative that encourages readability and evidence-based appendices that support believability.

As in the previous chapters, the views of other educators are offered to the reader as a balancing mechanism to encourage broader reflection of how and why a business plan can be productively used in EE. The aim being to ensure that its application is sound and appropriate to the strategic aims of the EE educator. That student output will not fall into a category of pure fiction bereft of real-world logic.

Chapter 11   Accounting for Interaction

The final chapter seeks to test the reader's capacity to remove themselves from their current teaching context; to step back and consider the nature of their teaching philosophy. The reader will be challenged to reconsider the ideas discussed in earlier chapters from some of the most compelling writers in the domain of education theory. Writers that lay bare our very purpose for stepping into the classroom,[18] who are advocates for the rights of our students to take control of their futures,[19] and who question the very basis upon how we know what we know when we study our classrooms.[20] Throughout this text a range of ecological ideas have been coalescing, introduced into a vortex that has been timed to unite within this chapter. To the extent that the reader is able to think about the ideas that have preceded this chapter, they will have developed a unique capacity to *think about how to teach EE*. The examples of the author's approaches to the dilemmas discussed within this text represent merely an example of how one person's teaching philosophy has been translated into a range of (constantly modified) learning activities. They do not represent a roadmap as to how to teach EE. Neither do the numerous insights from the many EE educators included in this text. This last chapter is an invitation to take up the challenge of campus ecology,[21] to sense the invisible forces that exist (regardless of our awareness) through which our students learning outcomes are so indelibly determined. Forces that can be imagined, harnessed and manipulated by the *thinking* and ever *reflective* educator.

NOTES

1. See for example, Jones (2006a) for a discussion on the development of the hic et nunc approach.
2. Based on ongoing work by the National Council for Graduate Entrepreneurship (NCGE) in the UK.
3. David Storey (2009) made several provocative comments about the societal value of EE during his keynote speech at the 2008 International Council of Small Business (ICSB) conference in Halifax, Canada. He questioned the assumed relationship between EE and any increased supply of entrepreneurs into society.
4. Bill Bygrave presented research at the 2009 Australian Graduate School of Entrepreneurship (AGSE) conference in Adelaide, Australia that demonstrated a negative relation between completing a business plan whilst studying entrepreneurship at Babson College and future business success.
5. Kevin Hindle (2007) convincingly argues that EE still has not developed legitimacy within the domain of higher education.
6. See Heath (1964) for a full description of the notion of the reasonable adventurer.
7. See Dewey (1922).
8. See Whitehead's (1929) seminal discussion on the value of educating in the student's *here* and *now*.
9. See Biggs (2003) for more discussion of ever present diversity in higher education.
10. See Gurin (1999).
11. See Hayward et al. (2009).
12. Within the context of this discussion an entrepreneurial journey relates to behaving in a manner contrary to prevailing (local) social norms to achieve an improvement outcome. By improvement, it is assumed the journey relates to the advancement of one's position or that of others in society, not necessarily dependent upon financial gains.
13. See Aldrich and Martinez (2001) for their discussion of resource profiles, specifically their explanation of the process of the entrepreneurial act.
14. See Hegarty and Jones (2008) for an argument that EE should not always be based on a business context.
15. See Lodish, Morgan and Kallianpur (2001) for an overview of the fundamental elements of entrepreneurial marketing.
16. English and Moate (2009) or see http://www.teaching-entrepreneurship.com/ideas.html.
17. See note 4.
18. See Palmer (1997).
19. See Baxter-Magolda (1998; 2004) for wonderfully insightful commentary on how students in higher education can take control of their personal development.
20. See Scott (2001) for an insightful critique of critical realism in the context of higher education.
21. See Banning (1978) for the seminal roots of the campus ecology school of thought.

PART I

Scoping the Issues

1. Your Teaching Philosophy

The justification for a university is that it preserves the connection between knowledge and the zest for life, by uniting the young and the old in the imaginative consideration of learning. (Whitehead, 1929: 139)

If you are looking for instruction on *what* to teach your students and *how* to do so, this book will disappoint you. If you are looking for help to discover just how important you are to your students' learning, read on. This book could just have easily been titled *how to allow students to learn about entrepreneurship*. Parker Palmer[1] said there is 'no question that students who learn, not professors who perform, is what teaching is all about ... [however] teachers possess the power to create conditions that can help students learn a great deal – or keep them from learning much at all'. Throughout this chapter, it is my intention to invite you to locate yourself and visualise the necessary journey from sage-on-the-stage, to guide-on-the-side, to meddler-in-the-middle that will aid your students' learning.[2] It is my hope that through understanding how my teaching philosophy has developed and influenced the learning outcomes of my students, you will gain entry to a place from which to reflect upon how *you* could teach entrepreneurship. Along the way, I hope you benefit from the introductions to the many educators who have influenced my approach to teaching entrepreneurship. First, some initial thoughts that have accompanied me throughout my initial nine years of teaching entrepreneurship. This chapter is therefore highly reflective.

I have always felt that entrepreneurial learning is not related to memorising external bodies of knowledge, but rather it is about self-recognition of internal knowledge. It is not always about events that are planned or predictable, but frequently about unplanned and unpredictable events. It is less about the knowledge of the educator, and more about the support of the educator. It is about the creation of what doesn't exist, rather than the maintenance of that which does. It is about freedom, not restriction, and it is as much about failure as it is success. These initial thoughts have accompanied me (relatively unchanged) throughout my short career as a teacher.

THE DEVELOPMENT OF MY TEACHING PHILOSOPHY

As a student I was disengaged, and an abject failure throughout my formal schooling. My grades improved once I embarked upon an apprenticeship as a diesel fitter due to the fact that it was vocational education relying upon my experiential learning. My father was a teacher and I observed his genuine desire to help his students to achieve their desired outcomes. By chance, in the shadows of a spectacular (and life altering) business failure,[3] I found myself faced with an opportunity to teach, having only just graduated with a university degree, believing three things: first, teachers should aim to help their students; second, all students should be fully engaged in the learning process; and lastly, teaching and learning need to be based on honest reflection from all participants. The immediate challenge to the development of my teaching philosophy was recognition of how all the *learning* bits related to each other. Figure 1.1 below illustrates my simplified take on the situation I was immediately faced with as a teacher of entrepreneurship.

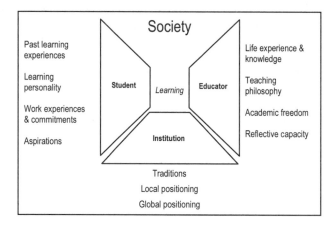

Figure 1.1   Simplified context of teaching in higher education

In the context of higher education, learning is situated between the interactions of individual students and the educators they encounter within a particular institutional environment. The learning environments encountered by students will vary markedly due to student participation, the nature of the subject area, educator contribution and institutional customs. Individual students will have different past life/learning experiences, differing learning personalities, differing work experiences and ongoing commitments and will hold different personal aspirations. The educators will have different life experiences and knowledge. They will undoubtedly have different (implicit or explicit) teaching philosophies. Depending upon the status they hold, they will also have varied levels of academic freedom and demonstrate differing commitments to personal reflection. Also, the traditions and local and global positioning of any institution will influence the nature of interactions occurring between students and educators. Finally, our colleagues and institutional cultures may hold vested interests as to how student–educator interaction should occur. Does this sound familiar? Given the dynamic nature of EE, the development of a desirable teaching philosophy can clearly be disrupted by several factors, many of which may not be controllable. The challenge is to understand where you are placed regarding your current teaching philosophy; generally a written statement of your approach to teaching that essentially remains forever a work in progress.

	Low Freedom	High Freedom
Low Legitimacy	A Target	On Borrowed Time
High Legitimacy	Are Student Needs Met?	Keep Running

Figure 1.2 Simplified context of your teaching philosophy

In Figure 1.2 above, a simplified context for the operation of your teaching philosophy is offered for your consideration. Regardless of whether you have or have not had the opportunity to formally write down your teaching philosophy, I argue that teaching entrepreneurship requires of us much vigilance as to how we protect ourselves from external perceptions of our teaching practices. If your approach to teaching has low legitimacy from colleagues who provide you with little freedom to do your own thing, you are a target for those that wish to stamp out acts of (perceived) deviance; persons that might typically prefer to protect their system/s. You need to achieve high legitimacy for your teaching practices. Institutional, national and discipline-based teaching awards are an obvious way of gaining such legitimacy. But without gaining more freedom, the needs of your students may still not be being addressed due to possible constraints by your peers.

Low legitimacy and high freedom is a better situation to operate in, but are you on borrowed time if your practices become known by all? Again the issue of legitimacy looms large. Only when you are free to address the actual needs of your students in a manner that has gained institutional legitimacy will EE be truly rewarding to you as a professional educator. However, even when you have achieved high legitimacy and high freedom, the challenge is to continue to do so. As you add more learning activities to your repertoire and encounter change in the workplace, the essence of your teaching philosophy will remain under threat. I have met very few educators in this field that feel totally free to operate as they please. Indeed, in a recent survey of international educators teaching EE (herein referred to as the IE Survey),[4] at least 50% of all respondents felt some constraint to the way they choose to teach entrepreneurship from their colleagues, school, faculty or institution. With reference to the development of EE at UTAS, let me reflect upon the development of my own teaching philosophy.

A Personal Journey

When EE was introduced at UTAS in 2002, my colleague and I decided that, based on the literature that we had engaged with,[5] a learner-centred approach would be most appropriate. We both had much start-up experience, but neither of us had handed the class over to the students before. It was nerve racking to begin with, but we could see that there was more potential to engage students by handing over responsibility for the learning to them than retaining power and authority in the classroom. Not long after we had started my colleague moved to another institution to start another EE programme. I was left to run the programme at a time when I had also enrolled in a Graduate Certificate of Teaching and Learning. So, a relatively inexperienced teacher, given increased freedom whilst also being increasingly exposed to educational theory. In reality, this was the point in time that my assumed components of a teaching philosophy came into contact with my first real reflections of what my approach should and could be to EE. Looking back, an iterative process of deep reflection (illustrated in Figure 1.3 below) has been continually occurring ever since.

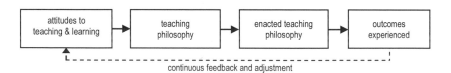

Figure 1.3   Iterative development of your teaching philosophy

Initially, the work of John Biggs[6] introduced me to many important ideas and provided me with profitable access to many seminal contributors to the educational literature. His process of constructive alignment enabled me to organise my feedback into three simple questions. What do my students need to learn? What learning activities would best enable my students to achieve the desired learning outcomes? And, what forms of assessment would allow me to know if the students have achieved the intended learning requirements? Given the complexity of teaching EE, I found this a simple, but challenging to implement process, a wonderful tool. It provided the backdrop to the development of my teaching philosophy.

My curiosity of the EE literature led me to the various works of Allan Gibb[7] and his notions that we as educators should create learning environments within which students experience the *way of life of an entrepreneur*, allowing them to walk in the entrepreneur's shoes so to speak. The notion that we should grant our students more freedom and ownership of their learning, that we should allow them to create their learning opportunities and use their social capital to reduce the risks associated with such an approach, seems very appropriate. At the same point in time, I also became aware of the work of Stephen Brookfield,[8] who proposed four critically reflective lenses through which one can view their teaching: autobiographies as teachers and learners, our students' eyes, our colleagues' experiences, and contributing to the theoretical literature. A hunger to blend discipline-based and pure educational theory was well and truly developing.

As my attitudes to teaching and learning changed, so did my teaching philosophy, and likewise the activities planned for my students. The next influential work I encountered was from Ralph Tyler.[9] Tyler asserted that 'learning takes place through the active behaviour of the student: it is what he [or she] does he [or she] learns, not what the teacher does'. To me, this represented a licence to get out of the way, to accept the challenge of Gibb to transfer more responsibility to my students. But it also required of me to better understand the process of how my students might benefit from such an approach. Observing the students reflecting on their behaviours between workshops and watching them adapt to *their* ever-changing learning environment led me naturally to use evolutionary theory to explain the process.

Thorstein Veblen's[10] work provided a means to consider how the students' habits of thought could be altered. Viewing the learning environment as the source of constant selective pressures, it was assumed that assessment processes would eventually favour those students most capable of adapting to the prevailing selection forces. I was less interested in whether it was the environment selecting for particular temperaments, or whether it was the adaptive ability of the students to changing circumstances that produced new habits of thought. After all, Veblen had expressed the view strongly that such processes had no identifiable starting or finishing point. He felt that 'the evolution of society is substantially a process of mental adaptation on the part of individuals under the stress of circumstances which will no longer tolerate habits of thought formed under and conforming to a different set of circumstances in the past'. The process was assumed to be an inexact process of adjusting inner relations to outer relations, made surer by the degrees of freedom surrounding the process, with student reflection a critical factor in the process. This ensured that the students had the opportunity to draw breath between workshops and contemplate what behaviours to retain, and what to add based on *their* assessment of the selection (i.e. assessment) forces in their learning environment.

The Inspiration of Whitehead

With my confidence growing as I fed off the feedback and enthusiasm of the students, I was introduced to the work of Alfred Whitehead[11] listening to a presentation by Kevin Hindle on EE. Impressed by Kevin's conviction as to the value of Whitehead's ideas, I obtained a copy of Whitehead's work and read it from cover to cover, several times. The ideas are breathtaking, and worthy of consideration by every educator, regardless of their subject domain. The key idea being that our students should learn in their *here and now*, that we as educators should identify the key principles related to their study and disregard all else that hinders their excited engagement and progress. In essence, *less is more*. Combined with the subject-specific ideas of Allan Gibb, my teaching philosophy became focused upon ensuring that everything my students did evoked their immediate interest in the subject area, that it exercised their mental capabilities, and that they exhibited such mental capabilities for all to see. I felt free, released by the wisdom of ghosts long past, whose ideas seemed timeless and highly relevant to my students' learning.

By this stage, the learning activities being prepared for my students were being radically overhauled from one teaching period to the next. New ideas from other educators met at conferences were being adopted and modified to suit the needs of my students. It was at this point in time when the legitimacy of my efforts was most under threat. I was operating in the high freedom/low legitimacy space, and I was on borrowed time. Two specific things enabled me to achieve legitimacy and scramble into a space where if I could keep moving forward, my teaching philosophy could remain in it's ever altering-form. The first was recognition at the 2005 Australian Awards for University Teaching, being named the Early Career Educator of the year. This award and its associated prestige created a lot of breathing space and essentially denied those that questioned the validity of my teaching practices a voice. During this time, I was also reflecting upon my teaching through conference and journal publications. This process helped me to build credible arguments as to why my students should engage in such learning activities, why they should take increasing responsibility for their learning outcomes, and why EE is different from traditional business school subjects.

However, during 2006 I was forced to accept that despite the general student excitement/engagement and the start-up success of a few students, the focus of my teaching practice was misplaced. By and large, my graduated students were not starting up new businesses. They seemed to be doing well with their careers, but were they entrepreneurs? I think the honest answer was no, from the perspective of the traditional usage of the term entrepreneur.

The most important implication to arise from this revelation was that my focus needed to be more on the development of the student, rather than on the development of their start-up aspirations; Chapter 4 will deal with this issue in more detail. During this time, I began to engage with the student development literature, starting with the works of William Perry, Robert Brown and Clyde Parker.[12] This led to the discovery of several works by Marcia Baxter-Magolda,[13] a champion of educational leadership in higher education. Her work on the concept of self-authorship seemed very appropriate to the domain of EE, and will also be further discussed in Chapter 4. However, my teaching philosophy, most influenced up until that point in time by the works of Allan Gibb and Alfred Whitehead, was slipped into overdrive through the unearthing of the relatively unknown work of Roy Heath.[14]

An Overt Focus on Personal Development

Whilst the opportunity for students to develop a business idea to market operation remains, a more general aim related to helping the students develop the attributes of a reasonable adventurer has emerged as the primary driver of their personal development. As discussed previously:[15]

> Heath defines the reasonable adventurer as a graduate student capable of making his or her own opportunities for satisfaction. A disposition argued to be a necessary pre-condition for engaging in entrepreneurial behaviours. Heath alludes to six specific attributes through which a student's ability to create their opportunities for satisfaction were enhanced. The first attribute is *intellectectuality*, the ability to alternate between being a believer and a sceptic. An ability to remain curious whilst determining what matters through making connections between the object under consideration and the reality of their world. The second attribute is *close friendships*, or the ability to discover the individuality of others. The realization that they have shared feelings with others and that prior

perceptions have been altered due to these friendships. The third attribute is *independence in value judgements*, or the ability to rely upon personal experience rather than known external authorities. This increased reliance upon one's judgement provides an avenue towards self-reflection that may be travelled with much vigour and enthusiasm. The fourth attribute is a *tolerance of ambiguity*, or the ability to view life as a series of interruptions and recoveries,[16] to be able to suspend judgements until sufficient information is obtained to make the right decision. The fifth attribute is the *breadth of interest* demonstrated. Heath calls this an uncommon interest in the commonplace. So depth replaces breadth to enable the sustained pursuit of specific problems. The last attribute is a balanced *sense of humour*. A benign, but lively sense of humour that distinguishes the reasonable adventurer, making he or she good company, and capable of being sensitive towards others across conflicting circumstances.

So a fully functioning graduate capable of using his or her individuality in ways beyond their prior mental endowments. A student connected to the reality of their world, yet able to find deep satisfaction from the ingredients of their raw life. Through the adoption of the reasonable adventurer concept, a new, exciting and obtainable minimal benchmark for my graduating students was established. One that would dovetail nicely into the creation of enterprise-related skills developed in the UTAS programme. Importantly, I had six attributes around which learning activities could be crafted and assessed. To lock in the potential gains possible from this approach, students moved beyond personal reflections to participation in a process of *group sense making*[17] through which they gained a heightened sense of their feeling and those of their fellow students.

The latest change to my teaching philosophy has been my recent development of a *4Cs framework* to further bring to life the ideas of all works previously noted in an authentic way. The 4Cs framework requires that within every entrepreneurship unit/module at UTAS, students must *conceive* new value, they must *create* it, they must *capture* it, and most importantly, they must *critique* their efforts to do so. I am trying to ensure they are constantly walking in the entrepreneur's shoes (Gibb), always in their here and now (Whitehead) whilst developing a sense of what they could be (Baxter-Magolda) through the development of key attributes related to their capacity to create opportunities for personal satisfaction (Heath) from an iterative reflective process (Tyler). My work as the meddler in the middle is continuously simplified through my ongoing reliance upon the process of constructive alignment to disassemble and reassemble the pieces of the jig-saw puzzle that is the entrepreneurship curriculum at UTAS.

Why this approach? I agree wholeheartedly with the sentiments of Professor Kazem Chaharbaghi[18] that entrepreneurs tend to be *found in society* more than they are *born into society* or *made in society*. As educators we have an opportunity to enable our students to discover themselves. At the heart of this thinking is an acceptance on my behalf that more than half of what our students need to learn resides within, that it is our challenge to allow a process of self-awareness to occur simultaneously whilst they walk in the shoes of the entrepreneur. Thus, I conclude that my (current) teaching philosophy can be stated as: *I wish for my students, the attainment of entrepreneurial knowledge that leads to entrepreneurial wisdom. I want my students to discover themselves in the lives they live. I want my students to be excited about learning and fearless of failing in the same breath. I want my students to be able to create opportunities for satisfaction within and after their university studies.*

Let us now briefly consider the evolution of the UTAS programme as contrasted to changes in my teaching philosophy (see Figure 1.4 below). From its inception in what I would now term a naive appreciation of learner-centred learning, my teaching philosophy has been continuously altered through constant exposure to the ideas of entrepreneurship educators and educational scholars. Throughout this process, an increasing importance has been given to personal and group reflection. Where multiple learning activities have been used, greater choice has been provided to students to account for individual differences, and the learning experience has moved as Allan Gibb would say, from learning *about* enterprise, to learning *for* enterprise, on to learning *through* (or *in*) enterprise. The current influences on the development of my teaching philosophy (and therefore refinement of the learning activities and assessment procedures used) are my developing appreciation of the application of critical realism in the domain of educational research.[19]

	Stage 1	Stage 2	Stage 3	Stage 4 (current)
Influences Upon Teaching Philosophy	Naïve sense of learner-centred learning USA EE literature	Blending of Allan Gibb's ideas with Whitehead, Tyler and Biggs	Personal/character development Literature (Heath, Perry, Baxter-Magolda etc)	The ontological issues related to assessing, teaching & understanding my students' learning
Learning Activities Typically Used	Task drive workshop presentations Large written assignment	Multiple activities aimed at student engagement, cases, games and group presentations	Multiple activities aimed at student engagement, cases, games and group presentations + more choice	Multiple activities + 4Cs (conceive, create, capture and critique)
Weighting and Focus of Assessment	Exam – 40% Presentations – 30% Reflection – 0%	Exam – 25% Presentations – 15% Reflection – 22.5%	Exam – 25% Presentations – 30% Reflection – 45%	Exam – 25% Presentations – 30% Reflection – 45%

Figure 1.4   Evolution of teaching philosophy and curriculum

At the heart of this unfolding process is a litany of mistakes and ill-conceived learning activities. Herein lies the ultimate challenge for the entrepreneurship educator: do you have the humility and courage to fail in order to succeed in helping your students? It is not possible to adopt an off the shelf curriculum from afar that will suit the needs of your students better than your reasoned development of a process that accommodates their specific needs. To do so outsources your primary responsibility as an educator, that being the determination of what your students need to learn. Put simply, adopting a text before you adopt a curriculum is selling your students short. Sure, be guided by many of the excellent works that have emerged in recent times, but do not allow yourself to become a slave to someone else's (possibly undisclosed) teaching philosophy.

The Context of Your Teaching Philosophy

I adopt the above stated position not to argue for the rejection of textbook-driven approaches to EE, as texts have a place in our domain. Rather, I seek to draw attention to a raft of dialogic relationships that surround the process of your teaching; relationships that will undoubtedly impact upon the development of your teaching philosophy and its enactment. By dialogic relationships, reference is being made to the fact that we cannot explain our students' outcomes without reference to our contribution and vice versa. Dialogic relationships exist between educators–students, educators–institutions, students–institutions, learning environments –educators etc. When you consider the context within which you develop your teaching philosophy, you must account for the many seemingly invisible relationships which may remain beyond your control. Clearly, such relationships will differ between educators in different institutions. Thus, what works for one, may not work for another. Yet, in adopting many texts and their prescribed content and suggested learning activities, we do so potentially without giving sufficient consideration of the dialogic relationships that have supported the development of such texts.

I invite you to revisit those texts, to seek out the authors' declaration of their teaching philosophies. Does it not seem strange that a body of work is offered to assist in the teaching of entrepreneurship without explanation of *how* this offering will allow our students to learn? The focus far too often is upon *what* the students should learn rather than *how* the students could learn about entrepreneurship. If we don't understand the various ways our students learn then we risk disengaging many by offering a one size fits all approach. This is an issue that will be addressed in more detail. However, let us briefly consider how colleagues in EE address the issue of teaching philosophies.

THE NATURE OF EE TEACHING PHILOSOPHIES

The IE Survey asked respondents to briefly state their teaching philosophy, their approach to EE and whose past (or current) work has most influenced their approach. Interestingly, not one respondent nominated a recognised educational theorist as contributing to their teaching philosophy. It would seem (see Figure 1.5 below) that it is very common within EE for teachers to be influenced by textbooks and the colleagues they interact with more so than any other external influence. If such a finding were to be representative of a broader pattern of behaviour globally within EE, it raises some important questions. Are our students fortunate that good teaching practices are being inherited through the texts and advice of leading scholars in the domain of EE? Or, is there an over-reliance upon the artefacts of other peoples' practice? While neither question will be answered here, the implications of each question should be reflected upon by the reader.

Parker Palmer[20] argues that good teaching is less about methods and more about the degree to which we as educators know and trust ourselves. That is there is a need to be vulnerable to the students and the learning environments we operate within. He further argues that we should avoid using artefacts (such as textbooks) to shield ourselves from the dangers we might perceive to exist in the learning environments we share with our students. But we wish to assist our students to learn about a truly complex subject, a subject that is rarely about objective facts typically found in textbooks. More commonly, it is learnt through experience and the use of imagination and reflection as encouraged by us the educators.

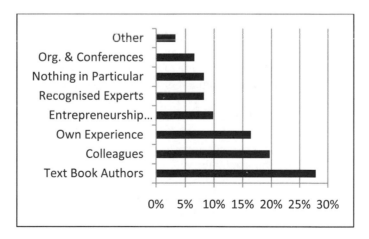

Figure 1.5   Sources of influence on teaching philosophy

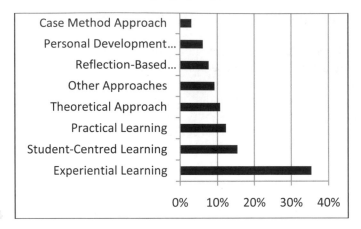

Figure 1.6   Types of approaches used to teach entrepreneurship

When asked to describe their approach to EE (see Figure 1.6), the IE Survey respondents identified several (non-exclusive) approaches to their teaching practice. Experiential, learner-centred and practical approaches are the most reported approaches to teaching EE. In reality, it is evident from the respondents' answers describing how they used their nominated approach, that various combinations of these approaches are frequently used to deliver EE. Let us now turn our attention to your teaching philosophy.

DEVELOPING YOUR TEACHING PHILOSOPHY

A statement of your teaching philosophy can be developed for various reasons. Increasingly such statements are developed to assist in gaining employment in higher education, gaining recognition of one's practice, or for gaining personal advancement within your institution. This section is focused upon developing a deep consideration of who you are as an educator, what relationships you wish to develop/maintain with your students, and ultimately how you will assist them to learn. Therefore, our focus is on an applied teaching philosophy for you and your students' advancement, rather than a documented teaching philosophy for your personal advancement.

In its simplest form a teaching philosophy should cover the essence of: how you believe your students learn; what you believe they should learn; what should be the impact of such learning; what activities they should engage with to learn; what type of learning environment is required to facilitate the delivery of such learning activities; how you will assess the nature of their learning; and how you will implement and monitor/adjust your teaching philosophy. There are many resources available online to assist you through this process of thinking about your teaching; but the most important resource is you.

To begin with, how do you believe your students learn? There are many cultural, institutional and individual (student) factors that will impact upon this issue as well as your own beliefs on the matter. Does your conception of learning relate to the memorisation of facts or does it extend to the development of wisdom? Is there a common process through which all students learn or do they differ in terms of how they learn? The answers to these questions inform you as to what you believe and/or accept within the conditions within which you teach. In essence you are working with your epistemological beliefs for they are the foundations of your teaching philosophy.

The next question is what do *you* believe your students need to learn? No one can answer this question for you. You know the context of their learning, of their situation within your institution. Are you involved in the delivery of EE within a team or do you operate by yourself? Do you have several units/modules with your students or just one unit/module? What is the overarching aim of your programme/course? Is it to produce entrepreneurs in the business start-up sense or is it to produce entrepreneurial types capable of dealing with the complexity of an ever-changing world, or both?

Next, what should be the impact of such learning? Are there types of students you believe your programme/course should be capable of producing? Are there some specific enterprising skills and/or critical thinking skills that must be developed to ensure the attainment of your desirable learning outcomes? In what ways might the students be expected to behave in order to succeed in your programme/course? How might this desirable form of behaviour differ from their other studies?

Next, what activities are required to facilitate your students' learning? How much legitimacy do your desirable learning activities have with your students, colleagues or faculty? Is there a change in behaviour required for the students to complete your learning activities? If so, how will you encourage trust from the student group to fully engage with the activities?

Next, what type of learning environment is required to facilitate the delivery of such learning activities? Do you require more interaction by the students? If you need to get out of their way, are they ready to take on more responsibility for their learning? Do they need to feel safe? How will you ensure they feel safe?

Next, how will you assess the nature of their learning? Will your learning activities create more assessable items? Will you be able to give useful and timely feedback? Will your approach to assessment fit in with the prevailing norms at your institution? Can you defend your approach if need be?

Finally, how will you implement and monitor/adjust your teaching philosophy? Who or what will provide you with feedback as to how successful your teaching philosophy is? Are there goals you can establish against which you can measure your progress? Have you a plan to reflect upon your development as an educator?

The above should not be taken as an exhaustive list of what must be addressed to develop your teaching philosophy. Your teaching philosophy is *yours* and will differ appropriately depending upon the various dialogic relationships that you operate within. The key is that you accept there is no real starting point; that has already occurred. There will never really be an end point, just many sequential points along the way where you can consciously adjust your approach as you search for continuous feedback of your approach.

In summary, this opening chapter sought to introduce you the reader to my own personal feelings of how I approach my students' enterprise learning. The aim was not to offer you an approach for you to consider the merits of, but alternatively to encourage you to reflect upon what you believe. I have attempted to convince you that it is through your own self-discovery that you will determine how you will teach entrepreneurship. That an over-reliance upon the standardised ideas of others will reduce your ability to identify and understand the particular conditions of your teaching that are specific to you and unlikely to be shared by others located in different contexts. To this end, the development of a teaching philosophy is argued to provide you with an opportunity to renew your interest in truly understanding your students' experiences of learning. My final word of encouragement on this issue is to reassure you that the process is made all the easier through working closely with your students. When students know you are interested in their learning outcomes and willing to explain what you are trying to achieve *with* them, an interesting thing can happen. First, they gain a deeper understanding of their required role in the learning environment. They sense what is required from them to gain the most from the experience. Second, they develop a sense of trust and belonging to the processes that are unfolding around them. They appreciate what is being attempted for them. Lastly, and most importantly, they become very forgiving of planned activities that fall short of expectations. I maintain that good educators will always push the envelope too far on occasions. In doing so, access to honest feedback is critical so that corrections can be implemented. I simply ask my students frequently how they are feeling about our progress during the semester and at the end of the semester I ask them what we should *keep*, what we should *add* and what we should *remove*. Throughout this process, being a teacher is fun and personally rewarding, regardless (within reason) of the outcomes being achieved.

Prior to discussing the central issues presented in this book, we will briefly detour to consider the history of EE, the current approaches and debates that are helping shape the space that we operate within. I hope you can continue throughout this book with an open mind, continually reflecting upon your feelings and the context you operate within.

NOTES

1. See Palmer (1997: 7).
2. See Erica McWilliam (2009).
3. Prior to becoming a lecturer at the University of Tasmania I was an active entrepreneur for many years building businesses in financial services, home services and the importation of farming machinery. Serious difficulties experienced with my home services (franchised) business led to a fall from grace. Staring at bankruptcy, I became a student of marketing and economics at the University of Tasmania to gain access to legal aid to seek legal remedy to my financial predicament. Eventually failing to avoid bankruptcy, I graduated and was offered a position as a *pracacademic* in a newly formed undergraduate program in entrepreneurship at UTAS.
4. The IE Survey is based upon the responses of 97 entrepreneurship educators from 35 countries and was conducted to assist the research process of this book (see Appendix 1 for details of the respondents).
5. See Jones and English (2004).
6. See Biggs (2003).
7. See Gibb (2002).
8. See Brookfield (1995).
9. See Tyler (1949: 63)
10. See Veblen (1925: 192).
11. The work of Whitehead (1929) has shaped my teaching philosophy more than other works I have encountered.
12. See Perry (1968), Brown (1972) and Parker (1978).
13. See Baxter-Magolda (1998; 2004).
14. See Heath (1964).
15. See Jones (2007: 230).
16. See Dewey (1922).
17. See Hart et al. (1998).
18. Professor Kazem Chaharbaghi, University of East London, Royal Dock Business School.
19. See Scott (2001).
20. See Palmer (1997).

2.   Entrepreneurship Education

In the context of higher education, how should EE be defined? The aim of this chapter is to consider past and current development of EE in higher education and to also consider a range of current practices and challenges that are set to shape the nature of EE as experienced by undergraduate students. It is not the intention of this chapter to provide the reader with any definitive definitions of EE, but rather to set the parameters for such discussion and to contextualise the different ways in which EE is discussed. Beyond this task, this chapter also seeks to introduce the reader to the perspectives of entrepreneurship educators from around the world. Let us first consider the fundamental issue of what is EE?

WHAT IS ENTREPRENEURSHIP EDUCATION?

There would seem to be growing support for the notion that EE relates to the development of *entrepreneurial capacities* and *mindsets*,[1] but less agreement as to what actually constitutes any such capacity or mindset. However, for some, EE is still tethered to the development of entrepreneurs who engage in start-up activities. Alternatively, other educators see EE as being more aligned to the development first and foremost of graduates with a capacity for higher-order thinking during these times of ever-increasing change. As will be discussed in the next chapter, there are major ontological issues that cannot be disconnected from our understanding of the purpose and nature of EE. Until we arrive at that particular discussion, let us stay focused upon what is currently offered for our collective consideration in the EE literature. I am drawn to the simplicity and breadth of Allan Gibb's[2] recent definition of EE as being:

> Behaviours, skills and attributes applied individually and/or collectively to help individuals and organisations of all kinds to create, cope with and enjoy change and innovation involving higher levels of uncertainty and complexity as a means of achieving personal fulfilment and organisation effectiveness. Enterprise education is the process by which these behaviours are practised and supported.

In provisionally adopting Gibb's definition, I do so to provide a navigational point for the forthcoming discussion, with the caveat of relying upon Tyler's[3] prior assertion that 'education is a process of changing the behaviour patterns of people. This is using behaviour in the broad sense to include thinking and feeling as well as overt action.' It is not the aim of this book to needlessly debate the merits of other competing definitions. As will be revealed shortly, there is something unique about the various works of Allan Gibb that sets his ideas apart from many other respected contributors in the EE literature. In short, he writes wholeheartedly from the perspective of the students' needs first and foremost, where others frequently tend to be anchored to the needs of educators and institutions. Let us briefly consider the history of EE.

A Brief History and Opinion of Entrepreneurship Education

It would seem there is universal agreement[4] that EE had its roots in the United States of America in the 1970s before finding isolated support in the 1980s/1990s in the United Kingdom and Europe, before emerging as a genuine course offering for undergraduates in the 2000s globally. Many factors are offered to explain the phenomenal growth in EE globally, not least the policy-driven notion that producing more graduates with enterprising knowledge and skills will 'unleash economic potential around the world.'[5] Students have also voted with their feet, seeking out course offerings that they perceive offer value within the context of the costs of acquiring their educational degree. However, it would seem that the fragmented nature of early EE offerings combined with the velocity of the field's development has resulted in 'a veritable pot-pourri of activity delivered under the enterprise/entrepreneurship umbrella.'[6]

Despite the rapid growth of EE, many questions remain unanswered as to what is its future direction. Consider the following issues that have recently emerged from the shadows of the last couple of decades of EE development. Prominent entrepreneurship researcher David Birch[7] has argued that it is not possible to *teach* people to be entrepreneurs, suggesting that they really need to complete an apprenticeship rather than a traditional classroom-based degree. He argues that the three fundamental attributes of an entrepreneur (i.e. selling, working with people, and creating products and services) are difficult to codify and embed in a curriculum. What if he is right? Might this mean that EE is more of a sorting ground where entrepreneurs are to be *found*, rather than *made*?

Recently, David Storey[8] (with reference to the work of William Baumol[9]) challenged enterprise educators to demonstrate the productivity of EE vis-à-vis stimulating the supply of entrepreneurs into society. Storey's primary argument, that Baumol convincingly demonstrates that throughout time the supply of entrepreneurs within society has always been strong. Therefore, why the need for EE when entrepreneurs have a way of always being *found* in society?

There could be little argument that the business plan has emerged as a highly utilised artefact of EE during the past decades. However, Bill Bygrave[10] contends we might collectively need to rethink its application within EE. With reference to recent research at Babson College, the success of past students in their current activities was deemed to be more related to their networking abilities (i.e. social capital), their ability to raise finance (i.e. financial capital) and their development of human capital (i.e. industry knowledge), rather than from the development of a business plan as part of their studies. Whilst an entire chapter will be focused on this issue, it does make you think about the path dependency of educator practices in EE. Is there a need to break free from the shackles of our recent history? If so, who will light the path forward? Will it be you, or will you wait for others to show the way?

With this in mind, it is no surprise really that Kevin Hindle[11] raises concerns about the legitimacy of EE as a source of value within the broader education community in higher education. He argues that it is down to us collectively to provide logical justification that EE is a feasible and desirable form of education in society. Given the high expectations of policy makers for EE and the various institutional challenges we as educators have in practising our craft, there is clearly a need to think about *why* we teach entrepreneurship and how *you* could teach entrepreneurship.

One only has to acquaint oneself with the most recent of reviews of the EE field to be exposed to the different perspectives held. In commenting on the field's past and future challenges, Donald Kuratko[12] provides a US-centric evaluation of EE that is seemingly tethered around the career development opportunities of academics. The plight of the student is seemingly cast as dependent upon a range of challenges all centred on the opportunities for academics.

Alternatively, Christine Volkmann[13] provides a critique of an EE landscape charged with the responsibility of producing potential high-growth entrepreneurs. However, in arguing for a comprehensive study of the EE field to determine what are *best practice* and/or *innovative new approaches*, the author potentially could be seen to be suggesting that EE can be reduced to technique. The educational literature is solid in its opposition that good teaching can be reduced to technique.[14] I contend that the problem is not so much knowing what other educators are doing, but rather knowing what they do without understanding the dialogic relationships that surround every aspect of their practice. Indeed, the European Commission report into *Entrepreneurship in Higher* Education[15] found the delivery of EE to be significantly impacted by the nature of internal organisational structures. So whilst Volkmann is correct to call for a detailed study of what is happening in EE, we must go beyond best practice to also research the nature of institutional structures and influences that shape such practice, good or otherwise. For example, consider Professor Luke Pittaway's[16] evaluation of the differences between EE in the UK and USA:

> Comparing entrepreneurship education in the United States to the United Kingdom is an inherently difficult thing to do. There appears to be as much or more variation between and within institutions and disciplines as there does between countries and these contextual features seem to me to be more significant. While I add this caveat there are some noticeable differences in entrepreneurship education between the two countries. In the US, entrepreneurship is a more established discipline, in some respects this makes it more stable and viable within institutions, while simultaneously making it more likely to be dominated by the pedagogic traditions of the Business School. I see more diversity in the origins of entrepreneurship education in the UK. It tends to be spread across more disciplines and in some instances is somewhat more embedded across the University. Another major difference seems to derive from the educational traditions of US business schools. While there are many examples in the US of innovative practice including many of the usual culprits (experiential learning; inquiry-based learning; service-based learning) much education is driven by text book based learning. In this pedagogic form the content of learning is led from a single text book, followed by appropriate lectures and multiple choice tests. For me this creates surface level learning. The tradition in the UK, while also demonstrating many examples of innovative practice, uses a lecture-based approach that expects wider reading on the part of students, uses more formative assessment (e.g. essays) and slightly less summative assessment (e.g. multiple choice tests). Neither of the two country's traditional forms of education is conducive to assisting the development of entrepreneurial capabilities and both traditions produce mindsets amongst students that take some effort to overcome when seeking to use more innovative forms of entrepreneurship education.

Again it is differences at the institutional level that most seem to matter. The recent *Developing Entrepreneurial Graduates* report by Herrmann[17] strikes a balance around a broader range of stakeholders through which EE is directly influenced. Vice-chancellors, faculty, educators, entrepreneurs, students and government meet at the intersection of *learning to be enterprising*. The influence of Allan Gibb's ideas is quite noticeable throughout the report, with emphasis placed on the need to shift away from learning *about* enterprise to opportunities to learn *for* enterprise. What is also noticeable in these recent commentaries of the EE landscape are the different challenges occurring simultaneously across the globe. EE is driven by different initiatives at multiple levels ranging from governments through to enterprise clubs and societies created by students to serve students. Clearly, any attempt to concisely capture the past, current and future trajectory of EE within a chapter is doomed to failure. However, let us push on to consider the nature of current practices and challenges that are presently shaping the EE landscape.

Current Practices

As noted, it is not possible to concisely capture the wide variety of learning activities employed by entrepreneurship educators; there are simply too many. The recent work of the National Council of Graduate Entrepreneurship does however advance our understanding of what activities are currently being used in EE. Their ongoing development of a *Compendium of Pedagogies for Teaching Entrepreneurship*[18] is an excellent resource for all educators in our domain. Adopting a constructive alignment approach,[19] the compendium is organised around seven distinctive learning outcomes (see Table 2.1 below) argued to be related to the development of an *entrepreneurial mindset* (or entrepreneurial person), rather than the sometimes more conventional notion of the graduate start-up.

Table 2.1 Learning outcomes related to the entrepreneurial mindset

---

- Entrepreneurial behaviours, skills and attributes including emotional intelligence
- Preparation for the 'way of life' of the entrepreneur
- Entrepreneurial values and ways of doing things, feeling things, organising things, communicating things and learning things experientially
- Entrepreneurial behaviour and management in different contexts – not just business
- Ideas harvesting, grasping and realisation of opportunity
- Managing entrepreneurially, holistically and strategically (know how)
- Managing and learning from relationships (know who)

In this approach, outcomes rather than inputs (i.e. focus upon marketing, finance etc) form the starting point of the teaching process. Outcomes that can be operationalised across a range of contexts/levels (see Appendix 2 for a broader explanation of the outcomes). From this perspective, a clear appreciation is being developed about the future potential of graduates to engage in entrepreneurial action due to the development of various enterprise attributes. Having offered a set of robust and flexible learning outcomes, the compendium provides an overview of in excess of 44 pedagogical approaches (or methods of instruction) that can be aligned to the above stated learning outcomes. The nature of this proposed matching process is provided in Appendix 2.

However, whilst there may not as yet be a consensus as to what is the actual purpose of EE, there seems to be a growing interest in the notion of developing the entrepreneurial mindset. Figure 2.1 below illustrates the responses from 97 educators from the IE Survey. Responses were grouped into eight categories that whilst different were also similar in many ways. Five of the categories (i.e. 90% of the responses) were related to positioning the purpose of EE as preparing graduates for what lies beyond their higher education studies. Interestingly, only a handful of responses explicitly ascribed venture creation as the purpose of EE.

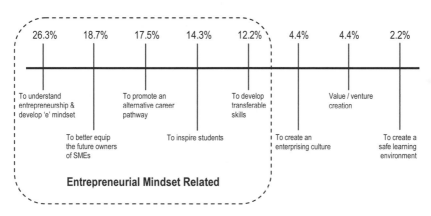

Figure 2.1   Primary purpose of EE

Figure 2.2 (below) highlights the pragmatic logic as to why such an orientation that is forward looking is necessary. Very few respondents from the IE Survey report the majority of their students engaging in start-up activities immediately upon graduation. This is an issue that will be addressed in greater detail in Chapter 3. It would seem that whilst EE will always be employed by educators and institutions for a range of reasons, it is sensible to appreciate a more general role in society of EE. A role that can be related to many local, national and international initiatives through the development of graduates with enhanced entrepreneurial capabilities. This is an issue that will be addressed in much detail in Chapter 4.

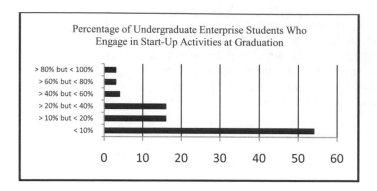

Figure 2.2   Graduates of EE and start-up activities

FUTURE CHALLENGES

The IE Survey also provided an opportunity for entrepreneurship educators to state what specific challenges they most felt the domain of EE faced. It was possible to group the responses into relatively discrete categories, categories that are nevertheless connected through the various dialogic relationships discussed in Chapter 1. Figure 2.3 identifies four emergent categories related to our institutions, our students, ourselves and the pedagogical approaches we employ. Let us consider each category, starting with institutional issues.

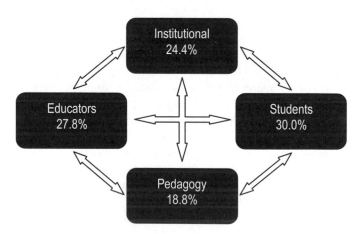

Figure 2.3   Challenges facing EE

Institutional Issues

There is little doubt that to many, EE represents a threat to other educators/administrators in higher education. It has been said that entrepreneurship is the last refuge of the troublemaking individual.[20] Take a moment to reflect upon the nature of those educators who passionately advocate new (and perhaps untried) methods to facilitate the delivery of EE. Previously, Weber[21] warned of *strangers* that continually challenge the legitimacy of the systems they operate within. Strangers destined to remain as strangers despite the fact they have the potential to add value to their community using their charismatic authority and determination to transform existing values and relational norms related to their community. Thus it is natural for our efforts to be frequently resisted, to be misunderstood and ridiculed. Therese Moylan at Dun Laoghaire Institute of Art Design & Technology in Dublin sees challenges from within a system that sees the delivery of education as class based and content driven. However, as noted by Professor Howard Frederick at Deakin University in Australia, all too frequently we encounter resistance from our universities, their deans and our colleagues. Given the potential broad application of EE within higher education, clearly we are collectively faced with development challenges. Dr Paull Weber at Curtin University in Australia argues that it is a lack of credibility within business schools combined with the dominant silo mentality that restricts the co-delivery of EE programmes, potentially preventing budding entrepreneurs within higher education gaining access to our programmes. The recurrent problem it would seem, as stated succinctly by Associate Professor Bennett Cherry of California State University in San Marcos, is convincing other members of faculty in other disciplines that EE courses are rigorous and relevant. Suze Strowger from the Ministry of Education in New Zealand also notes the need to address and debate any possible anti-entrepreneurship sentiments that can be held by some education professionals. In the meantime, David Austin of the Melbourne Business School in Australia suggests the need to develop the capacity to side step bureaucracy with agreement, in order to maintain forward momentum. Let us now turn our attention to the noted student-related issues.

Student Issues

The IE Survey revealed a range of educator perceptions as to why students find EE challenging, with the most dominant issue being the context of EE. That is, students not understanding the dynamic process of entrepreneurship and treating it as just another management subject. Dr Rob Fuller, Director of Entrepreneur Development Programs, Rady School of Management,

University of California, San Diego, argues that undergraduates often do not have a firm grasp of business, so have little context for entrepreneurship. Professor Luke Pittaway of Georgia Southern University in Savannah supports this notion, sensing that undergraduates lack any reference to their own practical experience. Associate Professor Jerry Courvisanos of the University of Ballarat in Australia concurs, offering the observation that students of EE frequently like the more prescriptive teaching in management and marketing, finding the idea of self-motivation (crucial in EE) difficult to fit into their limited view of the world. Many respondents noted the lack of desire in students to be responsible for their learning. Dr Robert Smith of the Robert Gordon University in Aberdeen hastens to remind us that many students come to EE in search of elective subjects and may not be particularly interested in entrepreneurship per se.

Clearly we face the challenge of attempting to inspire our students to be engaged, to be forward looking, and to better understand themselves in the process. However, for many students this is a huge shift in their attitudes and overall aspirations. Dr Kirk Heriot of Columbus State University in Georgia acknowledges his students work 30+ hours per week, his course is an elective accredited by the AACSB which requires students to work very hard using both sides of their brain; which really challenges them. It would seem that there may be a gap between the baseline aspirations and abilities of our students and the baseline aims and requirements of our EE programmes. Perhaps there may be a need to transition students into our EE programmes? Gary Palin, Executive Director of the Doherty Center for Entrepreneurial Leadership in North Carolina noted that today's students are quite often afraid of failure, many having not yet developed their creative side, and remain uncomfortable with ambiguity. However, the IE Survey revealed that the challenges we face as educators also emanate from our own failings.

Educator Issues

Perhaps not surprisingly, educators are confused as to what their role is in EE. There were a large number of respondents who indicated that they were isolated from mainstream education practices and who also felt that guidance as to *how* to teach entrepreneurship was limited. Monica Kreuger, President of Global Infobrokers in Canada, home to the Praxis School of Entrepreneurship perhaps captures the greatest educator concern; the disconnect between academia and reality. Dr Denise Baden of the University of Southampton in the UK raises the issue of the degree to which we can teach something that you would rather someone learnt. That is, the divide between lecture-centred and learner-centred approaches that still exist in EE. While this issue will be given much greater detail in Chapters 3, 4 and 5, it remains a highly problematic issue that goes to the heart of the teaching philosophy issues discussed in the previous chapter.

It would seem that the very vagueness and complexity of the entrepreneurship phenomenon is an issue for many. Gary Hancock of the University of Adelaide in Australia noted the ever-present misconceptions about what entrepreneurship means to our students, our peers and other educators, that is, *you can't teach entrepreneurs, they are born*. From such misperceptions it would seem there are many educators unsure of how best to approach their role given the usual challenges of large classes, and the challenge of what Professor Alain Fayolle of the EM Lyon Business School in France terms the 'complexity and heterogeneity of entrepreneurship' as a phenomenon. The last area of concern relates to pedagogical issues.

Pedagogical Issues

Beyond the housekeeping forms of challenges (student numbers and forms of assessment etc) the issue of our approach to teaching emerges as the primary concern raised by the IE Survey respondents. Professor David Kirby of the British University in Egypt succinctly states a need to reduce the dependence of our students upon their lecturers. A simple notion, but one that goes to the very heart of ensuring a learner-centred approach truly exists in the provision of EE. A desirable outcome that is not so easily achieved when the above challenges related to institutional pressures, the underlying capacity of our students as learners and our shortcomings as educators are taken into account. Dr Susan Rushworth of Swinburne University in Australia nominates the need to change student expectations that there are *right* answers and/or *single methods* for approaching a problem or situation. It would also appear that there are fundamental challenges that await us, with several respondents concurring with Professor Sandra Perks of the Nelson Mandela Metropolitan University in South Africa that we must ensure we succeed in linking theory to practice. Lastly, the 21st century sees us as educators cast as reluctant digital immigrants confronted increasingly by digital natives. Julienne Senyard of the Queensland University of Technology in Australia argues for the need of academics to learn about and apply new forms of social media (e.g. twitter, blogging etc) to address the ever-changing preferences of our students. At the intersection of the various challenges identified here are learning experiences created through the dialogic relationships that exist (sometimes unseen) between institutions, educators, students and the learning environments created for EE that link all parties. Let us take a moment to again consider the nominated influences IE Survey respondents identified as shaping their approach to delivering EE.

Past and Current Influences Upon Teaching EE

As noted earlier in Chapter 1, not one respondent nominated a recognised educational theorist as influencing their approach to teaching EE. In all, 97 educators nominated 78 sources of influence (including their own experiences/practices). The late Jeff Timmons was nominated by 10% of the sample, Allan Gibb by 7% and Bill Bygrave by 4%. Beyond that 75 others shared between one and two nominations. Clearly, just as we encounter enormous diversity in the students we encounter, so we do in the nature of sources of influence to our teaching practice. Is it any wonder that such complexity surrounds EE? One of the aims of this book is to encourage the reader to use their own cognitive heuristics to determine what matters and what doesn't. To allow a greater focus to be brought to factors that can be understood within the context of the reader's situation; to allow the reader to find themselves within EE and to redefine their purpose. To do otherwise would be to allow Bill Gartner's[22] elephant to remain in the room, continually prompting alternative viewpoints that reinforce confusion and prevent the development of clarity.

SO, HOW DO WE DEFINE EE?

Personally, I am drawn to the specific focus of Allan Gibb's definition presented earlier in the chapter … as a starting point. At this point in time, I might provocatively define EE as *a process of transformational education through which students are encouraged to better understand their capacity to create future opportunities for satisfaction through exposure to different learning experiences crafted from a learner-centred approach.* Why offer a provocative definition? Well, I offer it to encourage you to do the same; to encourage you to move away from adopting the positions of other educators/theorists.

There are simply too many permutations and combinations of teaching philosophies, institutional contexts, student types, course aims and educator styles to succinctly define EE in a universal manner. As educators we need to operationalise a definition of EE that accommodates our teaching philosophy, our institutional context, our course aims and, most importantly, our students' needs. This is your responsibility, and it should not be outsourced to those we might sometimes assume are wiser. No one knows you, your students and your institution as well as you do. It is important you can communicate clearly your definition to your students so that they fully understand what is required of them to participate in your programme.

What is being suggested is that we move away from definitions of EE that are assumed to be concrete to more localised definitions of EE that are context specific whilst still being consistent with other more overarching definitions. We will return to this issue in the forthcoming chapters. Now, we will turn our attention to the idea of the ontology of EE.

NOTES

1. See European Commission (2008).
2. See Gibb (2008: 106) for a contemporary overview of the EE landscape.
3. See Tyler (1949: 5) for a reminder of the classic ideas that accompanied curriculum development in the 1920s to 1960s.
4. See Katz (2003), Kuratko (2005).
5. See Volkmann (2009).
6. See Gibb (2008).
7. See Aronsson (2004) for a very insightful interview with David Birch that undermines much of the simplistic thinking surrounding the provision of EE in higher education.
8. David Storey (2009) shared his thoughts with me as to the central question that needs to be addressed regarding the relationship between the supply of entrepreneurs and their likely productivity and the increased provision of EE in higher education. Essentially, if we have managed to be served by entrepreneurs in the past (without EE) why won't we be in the future?
9. See Baumol (1990).
10. Bill Bygrave (2009) argues that a focus upon implementation plans may hold more value than assuming a business planning process will add value to our students' learning.
11. See Hindle (2007) for an impressive critique of EE in higher education.
12. See Kuratko (2005) for a useful overview of the EE landscape.
13. See Volkmann (2009).
14. See Palmer (1997).
15. See note 1.
16. Pittaway (2010), Personal communications.
17. See Herrmann (2008).
18. The *Compendium of Pedagogies for Teaching Entrepreneurship*, developed by Allan Gibb can be accessed at http://www.ncge.com.
19. See Biggs (2003).
20. This quote is commonly attributable to Nancy Clifford Barney.
21. See Weber (1968: 115).
22. See Gartner (2001) for a wonderful commentary on how blind assumptions can lead the development of ideas in our field astray.

3.   The Ontological Dilemma

If students of EE in higher education tend not to engage in start-up activities immediately upon graduation, how do we as educators determine our success? How do we know if what we are doing is worthwhile for our students? Within this chapter, I urge you to step back and take a moment to consider the nature of the assumptions that you may (implicitly or explicitly) hold regarding the nature of the reality of your students' learning and of your ability to know of this reality. Thus, this chapter places great importance on questioning what knowledge and/or other forms of realisable value might actually be gained from EE that can be used upon (or before) graduation. It is also important to understand why graduates of EE face unique challenges in their quest to acquire *specific knowledge* and/or *specific skills* prior to graduation. Let me first outline my ontological predisposition, so that you may better locate my thoughts relative to yours.

WELCOME TO MY REALITY

We all hold a position as to what constitutes the reality we operate in. Personally, I am a critical realist; I hold that reality whilst real can only be imperfectly known, and that it exists independently of any one person. I have previously[1] proposed that my students' *habits of thought* can be cast as generative mechanisms 'which are plastic enough to be self-altered through frequent reflection'. Mahoney[2] notes that generative (or causal) mechanisms are unobserved entities, processes or structures that act as the ultimate cause in generating outcomes. Therefore, I am content to live in a world where I accept that I am surrounded by invisible processes that (under specific conditions) give life to events that may not always be within reach of my appreciation or understanding. I am content to imagine such mechanisms and to contemplate their existence along with the nature of the conditions that relate to their operation and/or non-operation. So it is from the conjectures that arise in my mind that I postulate the nature of learning occurring within and between my students. Thus, it is from my own continuous empirical scrutiny that sense emerges as to how and what my students learn, as well as how I should teach, and within what environment such learning and teaching should occur. Figure 3.1 highlights the proposed ontological trinity of EE learning at UTAS. It is argued that three entities (i.e. the educators, students and the learning environment they co-create) interact in ways that result in the continuous alteration of each entity over time. It is the central presence of relational trust[3] that is argued to be at the heart of the interaction occurring between these three entities that influences the development of superior learning outcomes. Previously,[4] I have discussed such processes from the perspective of the creation of vulnerability. The processes surrounding such potential transformative change will be discussed in great detail in Chapter 5. For now however, the essence of such change will be contemplated from an ontological perspective.

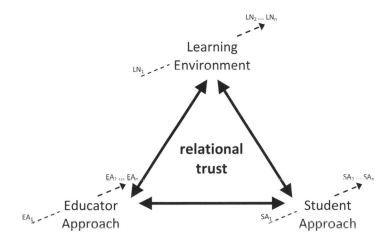

Figure 3.1   The ontological trinity

At the heart of developing the reasonable adventurer is a transformational process through which six specific student attributes are developed (previously noted as intellectectuality, close friendships, independence in value judgements, tolerance of ambiguity, breadth of interest and a sense of humour). Just how such attributes might be developed and how we might know their development is occurring are an ever-present challenge for the educator and/or researcher. Why might this challenge be ever present? Typically, educational research is based upon findings that are correlational, not causal. Therefore, it is not possible to say for sure whether it was actually the educator's performance or other factors in the learning environment that caused better (or worse) student performance. We can only conclude that students in such learning environments did better (or worse), but not necessarily why. Clearly, for the educator desirous of wanting to match specific outcomes to specific learning activities/approaches, a better approach is required. Let us briefly consider the opportunities to view this challenge through the lens of critical realism.

A Critical Realist Approach

Roy Bhaskar's[5] notion of the stratified reality of nature proposes that generative mechanisms can be separated from the behaviours they are assumed to create and from the events we experience as researchers in the empirical world. Stated another way, Bhaskar's stratified reality enables the educational researcher to separate the possible alteration of our students' *habits of thought* from any future expression of *enterprising behaviour* and our research of such behaviour at a *later point in time*. Therefore, critical realism offers an opportunity to establish a causal link between EE, the modification of students' habits of thought and altered student behaviour. Thus, it is the students' habits of thought that are assumed to be generative mechanisms that under specific (learning) conditions might be altered so as to produce (under other specific life conditions) forms of enterprising behaviour related to the notion of the reasonable adventurer.

Bennett and George[6] propose that generative mechanisms are ultimately unobservable social, physical (or) psychological processes that under specific conditions have the potential to transfer energy, information or matter to other entities. Bhaskar (as illustrated in Figure 3.2 below) argues that any such mechanisms are real and distinct from the patterns of events that they generate; just as events are real and distinct from the experiences in which they are apprehended.

	Domain of Real	Domain of Actual	Domain of Empirical
Mechanisms	√		
Events	√	√	
Experiences	√	√	√

Source: Bhaskar (1975)

Figure 3.2   Bhaskar's three overlapping domains of reality

When Bhaskar's notion of a stratified reality is introduced in this context, we are able to propose the possible presence of specific generative mechanisms (that are located in the domain of the real), to assume causal relationships between such mechanisms and altered student behaviour (observed as events occurring in the domain of the actual), and to account for contingent conditions associated with their operation and/or suppression (as we observe events in the domain of the empirical). A fundamental issue of Bhaskar's approach is his distinction between epistemology (or knowing) and ontology (or being). David Scott[7] notes that Bhaskar adheres to:

> Four foundational principles: there are objects in the world whether they are known or not; knowledge is fallible because any claim to knowledge may be open to refutation; there are transphenomenalist truths in which one may only have knowledge of what appears, but these refer to underlying structures which are not easily apprehended; most importantly, there are counter-phenomenalist truths in which those deep structures may actually contradict or be in conflict with their appearance.

Clearly, regardless of the paradigm of inquiry, we face a real challenge to acquire knowledge of the contingent conditions and structures related to generative mechanisms. Bhaskar's process of transcendental realism provides a useful research process through its use of the theoretical practice of retroduction. Richard Blundell[8] argues that retroduction 'involves the explanation of events in the social world by seeking to discern the structures and mechanisms that are capable of producing them'. The process relates to logically deducing particular historical outcomes or events – rather than testable hypotheses – from a set of assumptions. The aim is to find evidence about fundamental structures whose (assumed) powers act transfactually (i.e. in the domain of the real). Blundell argues that the process seeks neither to use deductive or inductive logic, but rather seeks (via empirical scrutiny) to progress from an initial description and abstract analysis to the reconstruction of the basic conditions that make possible the mechanisms. In essence, 'retroduction is about advancing from one thing … and arriving at something different'.[9] Let us consider an example of the process in action.

Conceptualising EE Value

A recent study aimed at determining what (if any) value was created from EE at UTAS was recently conducted by Matt Lansdell.[10] Matt, a former graduate of the UTAS EE programme relied upon his own cognitive capabilities to conceive (via reflection) what value might have been created, how any such assumed value could have been created, and the conditions under which any such value could be created and used to benefit graduates. His motivations for attempting such a study emerged from his post-graduation observation that many EE graduates at UTAS did not graduate as entrepreneurs (in the business start-up sense) but nevertheless seemed satisfied that they had

significantly benefited from their studies in EE. The notion of the fitting of
an ever-altering conjecture to an anomaly perfectly describes the process of
speculating about the elements of his proposed model of student value from
EE. At no point was Matt afforded security from the retroduction process,
merely the confidence to 'enter ... [a] ... skiff of musement ... [and to] ...
push off into the lake of thought'.[11]

Matt discussed his thoughts with a handful of other recent graduates with
myself, and eventually determined that the nature of value that was created
from the EE programme at UTAS was *self-confidence*. A seemingly simple,
yet potentially fundamental predisposition for any would-be entrepreneur.
Further, self-confidence is a central requirement for the development of the
reasonable adventurer. The process of retroduction used by Matt went
something along these lines. First, he stepped back and sought to describe the
events/activities related to the EE programme, paying specific attention to the
first-hand accounts of other persons and their various interpretations. In the
next phase of the process (having established the importance of self-
confidence as a graduate outcome), Matt sought to identify the various
aspects or components of any explanation for how any such self-confidence
was created. That is, given the development of self-confidence, what
conditions/structures relate to the development of self-confidence? Matt
identified (via a highly iterative process) the importance of 1) the educator's
attitude; 2) the type of learning environment; 3) the alternation of students'
habits of thought; 4) the development of self-confidence; and 5) the
mediating role of each student's resource profile.

Next, he considered what support existed across various literatures to
evidence his emergent logic. Next he sought to envisage the nature of how
his proposed model of Graduate Entrepreneurial Value would and would not
operate. That is, under what conditions should any such value be useful to
graduates and under what other conditions would it not? Matt then surveyed
graduates of the EE programme at UTAS from its inception in 2002 to 2008
to subject his proposed model to empirical scrutiny and gratifyingly
confirmed the underlying logic of his postulated model. That being; 1) the
extent that the enterprise educator is committed to a learner-centred
approach, has the freedom to be innovative and make mistakes and develop
open and honest relationships with and between students is central to the
development of; 2) a learning environment within which friendship and trust
are found, encouraging students to make mistakes and recover through deep
and meaningful reflection that; 3) leads to the development of the six
attributes (of the reasonable adventurer) and altered behaviours (i.e. habits of
thought) between workshops/semesters, and; 4) evidence of personal gain
across a range of social situations from value created (primarily) from EE;

and 5) evidence that a low/high resource profile was related to the likelihood of engaging in start-up activities.

Importantly, Matt was also able to explain the clear lack of start-up activity. Where graduates reported a low resource profile (at graduation), there was little evidence of start-up activity. Where high resource profiles were noted, there were high levels of successful start-up activities. An observed caveat was that higher resource profiles were also related to age. What Matt was able to demonstrate was that the EE programme had little impact upon students creating real social, human and financial capital. Alternatively, there was sufficient evidence gained to suggest that EE at UTAS was the primary driver of the self-confidence developed at the time of graduation. Clearly there are numerous implications that arise from Matt's study.

First, it is as if a magnifying glass has brought a clear focus upon the specific aspects of the EE programme through which value creation is *possible and explainable*. Second, the parameters of what the role of EE at UTAS should or could be have been questioned and the answers provide much food for thought. It would seem that despite the potential transformational aspects of the program, such change does not uniformly extend to the development of the requisite social, human and financial capital required to succeed as a start-up upon graduation. They require other forms of learning and asset accumulation that typically occur after graduation. Processes, however, that can be accelerated and/or sustained through the development of self-confidence during participation in higher education. Perhaps you might challenge that the surrender flag on business start-ups has been flown too early, that EE has been relegated to a minor role in the process of stimulating entrepreneurial activity in our societies. I would argue not, and will elaborate on this very issue in greater detail in Chapter 7.

CONTEMPLATING OUR ROLE AS EDUCATORS

I have commented elsewhere[12] that through considering EE as an ontological challenge, critical issues related to acquisition and use of enterprising knowledge and skills can be viewed in a different light. We cannot continue to place the cart before the horse. Delivering curriculums that assume the capacity for engaging in a business start-up immediately upon graduation without the prerequisite resource profile is at best a waste of time, and worse, a recipe for creating a sense of false capability. Perhaps we need to reconceptualise our role as the promoters of enterprising graduates. Given that by and large we cannot easily influence the composition of our incoming cohorts, and that we cannot control the genuine application of the developed knowledge and skills, perhaps we are the *cocoon* makers.

That is, we might consider the extent of control over the environment our students learn within, whilst acknowledging we cannot guarantee that they will sprout wings and fly upon graduation. If we are able to step back and consider what events must occur within the cocoon for a beautiful and capable butterfly to (eventually) emerge, perhaps we could better align our focus to this challenge. At UTAS, this process is referred to as the development of the reasonable adventurer. At other institutions it will be called something else and completed via different means. Let us consider what other educators of EE consider to be the primary value that is received by students graduating from their programmes.

Figure 3.3 below illustrates the various types of value that emerged from the IE Survey. Whilst self-confidence did rate as a nominated form of primary value, it was not a dominant category. That said, it must be noted that the groupings identified do not represent discrete groupings, but rather groups that could be considered to be positioned along an axis tethered by learning about enterprise at one end and doing enterprise at the other end. The most dominant grouping was those educators who perceived the primary value of EE as being related to developing *initiative* in our students, ensuring they take *responsibility* for their own learning, that they have the capacity to value *freedom*, and have developed a *passion* to pursue their goals. Lucy Kavindah in Kenya argues that EE students must understand that the most important resource in this life is themselves. In a similar vein, Charlotte Carey of Birmingham City University in the UK notes the ability to hone ideas and to recognise their own abilities. Or as Dr Jim Gazzard of the Royal Veterinary College in the UK observed that students need to become more proactive and effective in all aspects of their studies/life.

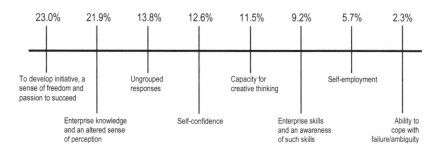

Figure 3.3   Primary value of EE

The second most dominant group related to those educators who suggested that knowledge about enterprise and/or an altered sense of perception of the reality of the world were of most value. Liv Dahlin at Oslo University College in Norway suggested that the value of EE is mostly about knowledge of problem solving, creativity, innovation and evaluation. Dr Alex Maritz of Swinburne University in Australia feels that value is derived from understanding the importance of the concepts and processes related to entrepreneurship. Many agreed with Dr Robert Morrison of the University of Texas-Pan American in the USA that learning to make a detailed business plan was of most value. Dr Griselda Correa of the Eastern University in Puerto Rico felt that the realisation of knowing what is important to be successful if they decide to start a business was of most value.

Skipping past the next group of ungrouped responses for one moment, the fourth largest group was that which related to self-confidence. David Austin of the University of Melbourne's Business School in Australia argues that students can get significant value from choosing to investigate possibilities that are wider than they had ever imagined might be available to them. Therese Moylan at Dun Laoghaire Institute of Art Design & Technology in Ireland felt that the confidence to also integrate their learning across subject areas was also important. Whereas Ted Sarmiento of Leeds Metropolitan University in the UK hastened to add that any such confidence-related gains might be undone due to over-confidence.

The next grouping related to the capacity for creative thinking. Professor David Kirby of the British University in Egypt argues that EE should produce creative, critical thinking and pro-active graduates. Associate Professor Jerry Courvisanos of the University of Ballarat in Australia associated EE value with the development of graduates who felt they could change the world for the better, if they act creatively to solve problems. Along the same lines, Monica Kreuger, President of Global Infobrokers in Canada saw the value of opening the students' eyes to their capacity to make change in the world.

The next grouping saw the development of enterprising skills and self-awareness of any such development as of most value. Dr Naomi Birdthistle of the University of Limerick in Ireland echoed the views of many in this grouping, arguing for the importance of students developing a self-awareness of their own skills and competencies. Gary Hancock of the University of Adelaide in Australia also noted the importance of developing openness and acceptance of the value of entrepreneurial behaviour, in others as well as self. Also, Dr Paul Jones of the University of Glamorgan in the UK spoke of the importance of graduates recognising they have the skill set to enable an entrepreneurial career.

A smaller grouping saw self-employment as the most specific form of value generated by EE. Dr Benjamin Okpukara of the University of Nigeria saw EE as a pathway to students creating a job for themselves. Whilst there are clearly contextual issues that influence the nature of graduate participation in start-ups, Nigel Adams of the University of Buckingham saw no reason why all graduates shouldn't commence a start-up during their studies in higher education.

The smallest grouping identified related to the ability of students to learn to cope with failure and ambiguity. But let's return to the ungrouped responses, where other forms of value are ascribed to EE. Associate Professor Pi-Shen Seet of Flinders University in Australia sees the source of value created by EE as providing an alternative to mainstream management education. Whereas Associate Professor Mark Simon of Oakland University in the United States sees the value of EE in that it allows students to rule in or out entrepreneurship as a career choice. Clearly the notion of what value is created by EE is a contested issue. But what is clear from the IE Survey responses is the transformational nature of EE. Without doubt, the respondents align EE value to outcomes dependent upon incoming students experiencing a form of education through which their values, attitudes, beliefs and confidence in themselves have been altered prior to graduation. But there is a tricky paradox at play here.

First, respondents to the IE Survey overwhelmingly did not consider it a problem that their students do not engage in start-up activities upon graduation. They sense a broader, more developmental role for EE. Second, adopting a development approach requires of the educator a very specific contribution. Let us interrupt this discussion with the addition of a syllogism designed to capture the challenge at hand.

> The primary value gained from EE is not derived from students engaging in starting up activities at graduation.
>
> The primary value gained from EE is derived from the development of enterprise attributes, skills and attitudes prior to graduation, therefore
>
> Enterprise educators must understand the nature of any such transformation in their students and how to assist and assess it.

To the extent that the logic supporting this syllogism is sound, the expectations upon EE educators are likely to be higher than on other content-driven subjects in higher education. The well-known educator Ralph Tyler[13] once contended that 'education is a process of changing the behaviour patterns of people. This is using behaviour in the broad sense to include thinking and feeling as well as overt action'. If this is the role as educators we desire then several implications that extend well beyond the possibilities of osmosis arise. Also, given that we are likely to be drawn towards the development of different types of enterprising graduates, our ability to operate in the domain of EE must be developed from within our own self.

It is upon this very challenge that the remainder of this book is focused. How do we as educators assist the development of enterprising graduates and how can we be sure that our efforts to attempt to do so are appropriate and/or successful? Given the nature of the idiosyncratic dialogic relations we as educators are confronted with, I contend our challenge is to master EE on our own turf. Not to optimistically import ideas from outside and assume they will work without modification to suit our teaching style, our students and the nature of the institutional context within which our students' learning environments exist. Before we embark upon this journey, let us again pause to reflect upon the nature of your ontological foundations.

WELCOME US TO YOUR REALITY

Are you inclined towards a positivist, critical realist, critical theorist or a constructivist orientation? Obviously, educators operating in the domain of EE will hold a range of views as to what constitutes reality. Many may have never contemplated this issue. However, to rise to the challenge noted above requires one to understand the world within which one *chooses* to operate. Karl Popper[14] proposed that there are essentially three worlds. *World 1* is objective and contains material things (therefore it is positivist); *World 2* is born from the subjective mind (therefore it is based on constructivism); and *World 3* is related to abstract things born from people's minds, but which exist independently of any one person (and is therefore related to realism). It doesn't matter which world you choose to live in, what matters is that you understand the nature of the world you live in vis-à-vis your ability to comprehend how you can assist and assess the development of your students. I noted earlier in this chapter that once we reduce our investigation to mechanisms that are assumed to alter our students' habits of thought, a critical realist approach is sensible if a determination of causality is desired.

In Figure 3.4 the three common scientific paradigms and their elements are outlined. How might you prefer to investigate the nature of your efforts to assist and assess your students' development? Would you prefer to approach this task in a value-free manner (i.e. positivism), in a value-laden manner (i.e. constructivism) or in a value-aware manner (i.e. critical realism)? As the investigator of such research, you must set your own parameters. Do you wish to know if there is an overall relationship between attending your classes and developing higher levels of self-efficacy? Do you wish to understand the various pathways your students travel upon to achieve their learning outcomes? Or, do you wish to isolate specific mechanisms that you

Scoping the issues

hold causally responsible for specific outcomes that are contingent upon the occurrence of specific conditions?

Paradigm

Element	Positivism	Constructivism	Critical Realism
Ontology	Reality is real and apprehensible	Multiple local and specific 'constructed' realities	Reality is 'real' but only imperfectly and probabilistically apprehensible
Epistemology	**Objectivist:** Findings true	**Subjectivism:** Created findings	**Modified Objectivist:** Findings probably true
Common Methodologies	**Experiments and Surveys:** Verification of hypotheses, chiefly quantitative methods	**Hermeneutical and Dialectical:** Researcher is 'passionate participant' within the world being investigated	**Case Studies and Convergent Interviewing:** Triangulation and interpretation of of research by qualitative and some quantitative methods

Adapted from: Healy and Perry (2000)

Figure 3.4 Three categories of scientific paradigms and their elements

Clearly, I hold a bias towards operating in World 3; that is not important. What is important is that you take the time to understand the implications and limitations of operating in whichever world suits you. As we move towards the next chapter, just be aware that it will be from my critical realist disposition that I speculate as to how I think about assisting and assessing my students towards becoming more enterprising.

NOTES

1. See Jones (2007: 230).
2. See Mahoney (2003) for a really useful paper on generative mechanisms and how we can explain their presence in society.
3. See Bryk and Schneider (2002) for their groundbreaking study on trust in the general education landscape, a much ignored factor in improving student learning outcomes.
4. See Jones (2009).
5. See Bhaskar (1975) for his seminal discussion of the stratified reality. For those who hold a more traditional scientific view, be patient and seek to understand an alternative world, where everything can't be known.
6. See Bennett and George (2003).
7. See Scott (2001: 14).

8. See Blundell (2007: 55) for a really useful discussion of the use of critical realism within entrepreneurship research.
9. See Danermark et al. (2001: 96).
10. See Lansdell (2009) for an innovative piece of research that had the courage to ask the most basic of questions: what value do our students gain from studying entrepreneurship in higher education?
11. See Peirce (1908: 95) for his highly seminal work of scientific reasoning.
12. See Jones (2010a).
13. See Tyler (1949: 5–6).
14. See Magee (1975) for a really concise and useful discussion of Karl Popper's three worlds.

PART II

The Nature of our Students' Learning

4. The Reasonable Adventurer

For me personally, discovering the notion of the reasonable adventurer was a very significant moment in my approach to teaching EE. Having previously dismissed most concerns as to *what* specific skills my students should be acquiring, my mind had already travelled forward to question *how* any enterprise-related skills should be developed. As discussed elsewhere,[1] my mind had become preoccupied with the question of how is it that some students are capable (more so than others) of coping with change, identifying and exploiting opportunities and being able to reconcile the known with the unknown? A question that is quite unrelated to any determination of what specific skills should be acquired. A question that ventures beyond the notion of which *skills* to also accommodate Allan Gibb's concern for enterprising *attributes* and *behaviours*.[2] Thus, a focus emerged upon what generative mechanisms might be involved in the development of the enterprising graduate? As noted in the previous chapter, Mahoney[3] views generative mechanisms as causal mechanisms that are frequently unobserved entities, processes and/or structures that act as an ultimate cause in generating outcomes. Within the context of this chapter, reference to generative mechanisms relates to the students' habits of thought (defined by Geoffrey Hodgson[4] as 'self-actuating propensities or dispositions to engage in particular responses or forms of action'), which are deemed plastic enough to be self-altered through frequent reflection. More on this process of alteration soon, but let us first get better acquainted with the notion of the reasonable adventurer.

A distinct challenge in the domain of EE is managing the expectations of students whose aspirations and general diversity are quite varied. The heroic notion of the graduate EE student preparing to battle for his or her slice of economic treasure soon faded with the disappearance of our first few cohorts of graduates. In its place emerged a realisation that setting expectations too high as to what was possible upon graduation was in fact having a negative impact on students. As their graduation approached, many felt as if they had under-achieved, that they had failed in their dream to graduate as an entrepreneur. What was needed was an intermediate step. Something that allowed the students to rest upon and admire their progress, yet not lose their confidence to move forward when they might deem it to be the right time to do so. Given the prevalence of graduates not engaging in start-up activities, this intermediate step needed some definite substance. It needed to be capable of allowing graduates to lock-in the gains they had made, and also assist in the preparation for as yet unknown adventures.

As luck would have it, I stumbled upon a little known study of Princeton University undergraduates by Roy Heath,[5] titled *The Reasonable Adventurer*. As I read his study from cover to cover, I found my intermediate step. I found a place to incorporate the ideas of Gibb, Biggs, Parker, Whitehead, Veblen and many others. I had found (as I would later discover) the perfect process through which to fashion my enterprise curriculum around and through. What could be more perfect for any EE course than to purposefully develop the attributes determined to directly relate to a student's ability to *create their opportunities for satisfaction*?

As previously discussed in Chapter 1, Roy Heath's notion of the reasonable adventurer is built around six specific attributes: 1) *intellectectuality*; 2) *close friendships*; 3) *independence in value judgements*; 4) *a tolerance of ambiguity*; 5) *a breadth of interest*; and 6) *a sense of humour*. Let us briefly again consider the nature of each attribute and mull over a selection of student comments from my past students who have been exposed to a curriculum built around these attributes.

Intellectuality

In work that presents modern-day similarities to Heath's past research, Baxter-Magolda[6] proposes a self-development concept she describes as *self-authorship*. Her work outlines a journey of self-discovery through which three specific dimensions, the epistemological, intrapersonal and interpersonal, are considered. In an earlier work, Baxter-Magolda[7] defines self-authorship as 'the ability to collect, interpret, and analyse information and reflect on one's own belief in order to form judgements'. Thus, Baxter-Magolda is also championing the importance of being able to alternate between a *believer* and a *sceptic*. It is interesting to reflect upon some of my students' comments regarding this attribute.

> I am not really sure if I have developed the ability to alternate between the two. Maybe I already had the ability and I have developed it further. I probably am a bit more of a believer in some ways, and then I get more sceptical by talking to other people. By discussing things in a group, with my group members it does bring in different views, even in the way I understand things, so it introduces a bit of scepticism just by discussing the meanings between different people from different backgrounds. (student comment no. 1)

Well to be honest I think the unit has probably swung me towards being a believer more so than a sceptic. I can alternate between the two, but starting off I would have been a pretty strong sceptic. I wouldn't say I am a negative person, but I'm just a very cautious/careful person by nature. The failure that many entrepreneurs encounter had put me into the sceptic category to start off with, but I began to believe a lot more towards the end of the unit, and I really love the phrase 'you will miss 100% of the shots you don't take', it's just so true. (student comment no. 2)

I think I have always been more of a sceptic than a believer depending on the situation of course. My ability to balance these two mindsets I feel has improved during the semester and because of this I feel that I have become a better analyst. (student comment no. 3)

I feel as if I have always had the ability to be both a believer and a sceptic; entrepreneurship has opened my eyes to the fact that it's good to be a believer. (student comment no. 4)

I sense that the above presented student comments indicate that students may tend to start from a position of scepticism, that perhaps they have lost faith with the educational systems they encounter. Perhaps it is exposure to lecturers who preach from a text without conviction (or connection to the students' reality) that has caused a loss of faith in their own abilities as learners? What is not in doubt is that by bringing a deliberate focus upon the needs of the students to decide what is true and what is not, they have become more responsible for their own learning; a necessary precondition of student-centred learning.

Close Friendships

The next attribute is that of close friendships, or the ability to discover the individuality of others. Or, the realisation that they have shared feelings with others and that prior perceptions have been altered due to these friendships. Again, the voice of the students is very interesting.

Yeah I think it's fantastic I have a rather multicultural group. I probably never would have met such a great group of people. Being from different cultures it points out how different and individual we all are. Different people in my group are better at different things, and I think that we make a good team because we have that variety amongst us. Out of all the groups I have worked with this semester, my entrepreneurship group has become my closest friends…and who could've ever guessed that. We are all so different yet we still have things in common. (student comment no. 5)

Although I know XXX pretty well, I actually appreciate the way we can so easily work on a task together, he's better in the technical/conceptual area and I'm better in the style/presentation area. I really appreciated this when we put the last presentation together, it was just so easy to work with these different skills. (student comment no. 6)

Without the others, we never could have variation in our presentations. As an individual you think in one pattern and combining that with my group members made us take roads that we never would have explored without each other. I like group work, brainstorming for a group work is the first step to being creative and the individuality of others couldn't be more important. (student comment no. 7)

Each member of my group has their own unique qualities, and it's been fun to get to know each one. Before XXX was introduced to the group, it was easy for all of us to get things done quickly and we had a lot of fun doing this. We all got to know one anothers' humour, and ways of doing things – and I was comfortable, but when XXX was introduced to the group, things changed a little and I had to make sure (as a group) we were taking things slower and making things clearer (as she is an international student with not very good English). I definitely developed an appreciation of the individuality of XXX, she was so good at getting involved – and I found it amazing how she was so patient. I know I wouldn't be if I was in her situation. (student comment no. 8)

During this semester I was involved in a very effective and productive group ... the entrepreneurship course did not require everyone to think the same or say the same thing like many other uni courses ... this was a major factor with regards to our group's success and greatly helped us develop an appreciation of each others' individuality. (student comment no. 9)

An explicit focus upon group work is increasingly being developed to foster close working relationships. It would seem that students have found this form of learning very supportive in terms of developing new friendships, and developing a greater appreciation of others. Given the importance of developing future social capital and network ties, this would appear an excellent outcome for the students. Perhaps most pleasing has been the integration of international students with Australian students, and their willingness to take the time to appreciate their cultural differences.

Independence in Value Judgements

The third attribute is *independence in value judgements*, or the ability to rely upon personal experience rather than known external authorities. Once again, the student voice provides an interesting lens as to the value of the learning activities within the unit.

I am more confident that my thoughts and frame of reference actually have substance and are contributing to my decisions. I have always relied on others for feedback in assignments etc, but here I don't have anyone that close to trust so I have to rely on myself and my judgement. (student comment no. 10)

I guess this unit is so different to other units that I've done, it's hard to rely on experience. The case study discussion is an example of that, because I've never really done anything like that before, it's hard to relate other past experiences I've had to it. So I guess in a sense some basic experiences that I've had have helped make simple decisions, but overall I've had to adapt and learn in order to make decisions. (student comment no. 11)

I very much tend to focus more on trying to stick to the academic guidelines as opposed to taking risks with things. This was true in terms of the game, where I never played the risky option. I always went with what seemed like the right answer. On a lot of occasions I got this right but I guess it didn't really pay off because of all the others taking risks. (student comment no. 12)

I did have to rely on personal experiences when completing the assignment and these reflective journals, more so than in other units I have completed at university. (student comment no. 13)

Well this unit has definitely been different to any other one that I have done before and I have to say that it threw me a little bit at the beginning, definitely wasn't what I was expecting. I guess I have relied on my personal experience through this unit, especially with the presentations, as I really had no knowledge of the content at all. It's taken a while but I've become less confused than I was at the beginning and this unit has definitely pushed me outside my comfort zone. (student comment no. 14)

With regards to this attribute, student opinion seems somewhat more divided. My personal observation is that the extent to which a student is accommodated within a well-functioning group matters. When the group functions on the basis of listening to and appreciating the individuality of each member, students tend to increase in confidence. Confidence that I perceive allows them to take greater responsibility for their eventual decision making. When the opposite is true, students may default to a position of looking for an institutional *rule* or *position* to adopt. Comment 14 is interesting in that the student in question was in a dysfunctional group and didn't manage to catch on to an entrepreneurial way of thinking. This perhaps suggests that as educators, we must pay attention to ensuring the micro foundations of group work are sufficient to stimulate and not stymie entrepreneurial thought.

Tolerance of Ambiguity

A *tolerance of ambiguity* is the fourth attribute, or perhaps as Dewey[8] noted, the ability to view life as a series of interruptions and recoveries. Stated a little differently, the ability to be able to suspend judgements until sufficient information is obtained to make a more informed decision.

I'm the kind of person who likes to be organised and know what is happening and expected and most importantly, I like to understand what I am doing. I have had some frustration this semester with not understanding things, especially the game. But as the semester has progressed I have been able to handle that better, I don't think that I have been all that worried about it and in some ways I've found it better as I haven't been stressing about this unit or the marks as much as other units, I've just been having fun. I still don't like not understanding things but I believe I have gotten better at dealing with it. (student comment no. 15)

I don't think I'm the kind of person who likes to have their outcomes based on others people's willingness to show up to meetings or their creative intelligence. I like to think if I do badly at something, it's because I haven't worked hard enough for it. For a lot of this unit it was not the case and it frustrated me often. (student comment no. 16)

I have felt myself becoming frustrated at times throughout the semester with circumstances where there has been ambiguity. I am the type of person who will strive to do the best that I possibly can and get frustrated by anything that stands in the way of an effective or efficient process. I can now see that while at the time, this ambiguity seemed to be a real nightmare; it has actually increased what I have learnt because of the reflection and thinking time that ambiguity stimulates. (student comment no. 17)

I dislike ambiguity; with regards to reasoning and decision making I need things to be clear and precise with reasonable structured reasoning behind it. Although I did not gain a greater tolerance of ambiguity I feel as if I have enhanced my people skills through asking questions and more open communication. (student comment no. 18)

Student comments regarding the development of a tolerance for ambiguity reveal that whilst some students are relatively flexible, some are very rigid when it comes to compromising their academic outcomes and developing an ability to suspend judgement. Whilst not surprising, this issue nevertheless remains an important one when educators are committed to creating a learning environment free of naysayers. Studies in EE at UTAS typically represent a departure point for the way in which students approach their studies. As such, more work is required to ensure those more pessimistic students who perhaps are more risk adverse are stimulated to relax and go with the flow.

Breadth of Interest

Building on Whitehead's[9] notion of ensuring that our students learn in their here and now, the fifth attribute was easy to accommodate. Students in groups were provided with a reading before each new workshop. Their challenge; to explain the central idea in the reading as it relates to their lives.

Heath calls this an uncommon interest in the commonplace. So depth replaces breadth to enable the sustained pursuit of specific problems.

> This unit seems to be very focused on the way different people act in different ways, in different situations and for different reasons. I have found that most of the theory seems way more complex than it really is and by applying it to more mundane or simple situations, it has allowed me to generate a better understanding of it more quickly. (student comment no. 19)

> I really enjoy the fact we were encouraged to apply the theory to our own lives. It made it easier to understand the key ideas, and we also got to see how the other groups made sense of the ideas in their lives. (student comment no. 20)

> Initially I felt ripped off, the lecturer was not telling us anything, and we were the ones doing all the work. Then we started to have fun creating our presentations. We started to really look forward to seeing the presentations of the other groups. Then I realised we had been tricked into a different way of learning. (student comment no. 21)

While I place equal importance on each attribute and consider each one germane to the development of each student, I must admit a soft spot for this attribute. Why is this so? We had been asking students to discover a connection to the theoretical ideas in their own lives long before I found the notion of the reasonable adventurer. It just fitted in like the last piece of a complex jig-saw puzzle.

Humour

Perhaps my gravitation towards the use of humour in the classroom to sweeten the relationships between all who engage in EE at UTAS is a reflection of my own approach to life. I would like to hope that I have always approached life in the spirit of the saying, *never attribute to malice what can be adequately explained by stupidity*. Thus, I have encouraged my students to err on the side of benign humour rather than take life too seriously.

> Yeah this has been fantastic. It's a great way to learn. I have really enjoyed doing this kind of thing. It brings the fun back into life, and that is what it should be about. Too many people seem to think that we should have to do it hard. It appears some of the lecturers go by the notion that they had to do it the hard way and so should we. But it's so much more effective this way, if you can learn and be assessed in a way in which you enjoy then it's a skill you can keep for life. Because essentially we need to learn skills for life, so we can do a job at the end of all this, not just know the theory, but physically be able to apply it. I have had great fun with my group, we always find that we spend half the time doing our presentations laughing our heads off... it's more enjoyable and so much less stressful! I guess I am just lucky to have had such a great group of people to work with. (student comment no. 22)

Yes, I enjoyed the humour within the class, it just makes the class not boring and it's really good to be able to laugh and enjoy it. The other groups probably used the humour thing a lot more with the sock puppets and other things they did more so than our group. But I think putting together presentations in our group we just had such a great time, the other guys were great to work with and real larrikins, even in the discussions about how we could put it together we'd joke about it and examples we could use. I remember when Alex came around to my place to help me work on the presentation when Tom couldn't make it and I was showing him the video clip saying how we were going to use it and he thought I was joking about it and freaked out when we told him we were serious and we all had a laugh and explained how exactly we could use it. Outside the group activities the use of humour was good to communicate with, I liked the way it was used in the case study discussion as a way of getting from the start to the end results. (student comment no. 23)

Ask anyone in our group what they think of me? I'm sure it will have something to do with hyperactive, constantly silly etc. I think humour plays a major role in all group activity, and you can see the results of using it – a happier and cohesive group. Also when reflecting on all groups' presentations, humour has been used extensively, allowing for the whole class to enjoy the benefits of it. (student comment no. 24)

I thought within my group, humour was the most common form of communication. My group was hilarious to work with, every single member was humorous in their own way, and a lot of the time without even realising. Outside group activities I also used humour with quite a few people. I realised the rest of the class was also quite humorous, which I think, made this class a lot of fun and I really enjoyed it. (student comment no. 25)

These comments are very representative of the general feedback from students studying EE at UTAS. They constantly support the notion that humour was a great ice-breaker. That it facilitated student interaction and provided a quick route towards the attainment of self-confidence in the learning environment. I have previously noted that regarding my own childhood learning, the presence of fun was an important element in my own learning. The use of humour would appear to have engendered a *Sesame Street* factor, whereby students who are drawn to the excitement and fun of the learning activities become fully engaged, and once they enter their post-workshop reflective phase, acknowledge a learning gain.

THE REASONABLE ADVENTURER AS ENTREPRENEUR?

The same students who supplied the above presented quotes were also asked to consider what they learnt about themselves vis-à-vis their future potential to engage in entrepreneurial behaviour. Their responses were very interesting.

> At the end of the day I am very proud of myself for how far I've come, with everything changed around me during the semester I definitely have a greater tolerance for ambiguity and instead of letting a bad situation get the better of me I became more determined to keep going. You can't succeed unless you're willing to fail, I can definitely relate to that sentence now, and looking at the changes I have brought about in my own environment at home with 'positive deviance' and at school in my group. I know that I can do it if I try! (student comment no. 26)

> One thing that I learnt about myself this semester was that I am very motivated to achieve – I am not saying that this unit made me develop awesome motivation, but I feel it made me look at myself in relation to some of the entrepreneurs I read about and say to myself, yes, I would persist in that situation like they did. I think persistence is important in order to achieve entrepreneurial success. (student comment no. 27)

> This semester what I have learnt about engaging in entrepreneurial behaviour is if it is anything like the group activities we did in class, then I am not cut out for it. I guess the main issue that stands out to me is my inability to control situations. For example, the game was based on luck and the group composition was based on where you sat in the first class. As it turns out I really didn't like not having control over things that could be important. (student comment no. 28)

> The reason I loved this unit was because as students we were given the reins; we are given the freedom of expression and at the same time we are given a great responsibility of teaching one another, of exploring better ways of doing it, engaging with each other. All of these factors I have thrived on, as I have realised all semester that this six month period of my life was a bridge between education and the workforce. (student comment no. 29)

There is a great sense of empowerment, freedom and reflection in all the above comments. Whilst no approach can ever claim to be the best way to create enterprising graduates, I think we need to accept that we are all capable of developing our own successful approaches. The key is to find benchmarks to measure your creations against. For my mind, the work of Allan Gibb provides many such benchmarks.

Allan repeatedly calls upon educators in the EE domain to recreate the *entrepreneurial way of life*. What seems lost on many new educators entering the EE domain is that Gibb does not say *how* this should be done, only that it *should* be done. The how is our challenge; a challenge shaped by the nature of dialogic relationships we constantly wrestle with. In an earlier contribution, Gibb outlines 14 pedagogical challenges to recreating the entrepreneurial way of life. The challenges can be summarised as developing: 1) commitment; 2) a strong sense of responsibility; 3) a strong sense of ownership; 4) a capacity to cope with risk; 5) a capacity to cope with long hours; 6) a sense of freedom; 7) a capacity to make decisions under uncertainty with limited data; 8) an ability to manage stakeholder relations; 9) a capacity to take initiatives; 10) an ability to manage financial capital fluctuations; 11) an ability to manage changes in social relations; 12) a capacity to manage/control holistic tasks; 13) a capability to learn to learn by doing and reflecting; and 14) a capacity to cope with loneliness.

Our test as educators (if we choose to use such a set of challenges) is to contemplate what learning activities would lead to the required skill development to develop such capacity and/or ability in our graduates. As discussed in Chapter 1, this is a task that cannot be outsourced. It is within this challenge that we live or die as EE educators. The good news is that there are no totally correct ways to do it, only various contested combinations of learning activities that can be assembled, disassembled and reassembled to move us closer to developing a desirable set of enterprising skills.

Clearly however, there are few guarantees that either, 1) we can develop any such desirable skill set in each and every graduate, and 2) that we as educators can implement a programme that will always achieve designed outcomes. However, this does not prevent universities from guaranteeing that undergraduates will have the opportunity to attempt such self-development. On the basis that such skill development outcomes are both determined and desirable, the next question remains as to how any such skills are developed.

DEVELOPING ENTERPRISING SKILLS

Delving back into the issues discussed in the previous chapter, we can now consider in more detail how we can actively assist in the development of skills. I have discussed these ideas previously and they potentially create a challenge to the reader. Let me try my best to explain my ideas on how my students' skill development occurs. Figure 4.1 below at first glance may appear quite complex. The underlying philosophy behind the process illustrated in Figure 4.1 is related to Geoffrey Hodgson's[10] notion of Lamarckian evolution nested within a Darwinian process of modification by descent (i.e. moving from left to right).

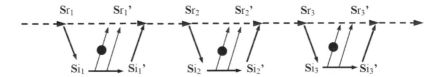

Figure 4.1   Interacting and replicating entities

A Darwinian theory concerns the process of change, assigning the major (but not exclusive) causal role to natural selection. The presence of Lamarckism is granted on the basis that 'acquired characters are inherited only rarely and weakly' relative to the process of natural selection.[11] That is, a Lamarckian process can nest within the overarching nature of Darwinism, assuming that we accept that social entities can acquire (heritable) characters in a metaphoric sense.[12]

Let's work our way through Figure 4.1. From left to right, there are a series of connected broken arrows that represent the journey of the student across time. Above and below this set of broken arrows are letters (Sr or Si) marked with an 'r' to indicate replicating entities, and 'i' to indicate interacting entities. The movement from left to right illustrates the change in both replicating and interacting entities. So as not to prolong any confusion at this point, let's recap before going further. Figure 4.1 illustrates the change in a student's habits of thought across a period of time. As previously noted,[13] the habits of thought are 'self-actuating propensities or dispositions to engage in particular responses or forms of action'. This explanation of change uses a focus upon replicating and interacting entities. In Figure 4.1, solid arrows indicate causal relationships related to the process of student development (via natural selection). The twin (upward facing) arrows indicate the acquisition of acquired characters (i.e. modified habits of thought as previously defined). One of the arrows has a small black circle on it signifying the acquisition of skills; the other arrow signifies the acquisition of knowledge (or ideas). Let us first break down the underlying causal process in further detail before explaining the suggested process further.

The symbol 'Si' refers to the students' interaction with all elements of the learning environment. The symbol 'Sr' refers to the students' repertoire of habits that whilst relatively stable are plastic enough to be altered through frequent interaction inside and outside of the learning environment. Thus, we are concerned with the students' habits of thought (or replicating entities) that are able to be modified through interaction with all other elements of the learning environment. The selection process is formally achieved via the methods of assessment used that are designed to reward particular forms of enterprising behaviour, and informally via student reflection of one's own performance.

What is being suggested therefore is a process of enterprise skill development via separate processes of natural selection (or the assessment) and internal selection (such as student reflection) that are complemented by acceptance of the inheritance of acquired characters. Figure 4.1 illustrates a timeframe related to three workshops, although in reality there would typically be more. As each student interacts with their group the first time (Si_1 to Si_1'), their individual performance will initially be determined by each student's habits of thought (e.g. their capacity to communicate, think creatively, etc), and to a lesser degree by the traits they acquire through their interaction with their group and other groups. Consequently, each group also has the ability to inherit acquired characters (or skills) through individual learning and from copying the behaviours of others. As this occurs, the replicating 'code' of the students (and their groups) is subject to change that may (or may not) prove beneficial going forward to the next workshop. Let's view this process from the perspective of group work to offer another way of understanding the process.

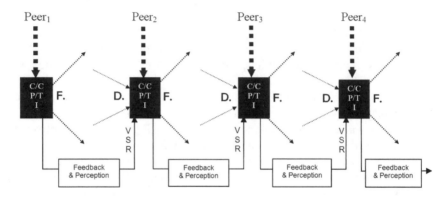

Figure 4.2   Habits of thought modification and student presentations

In Figure 4.2 above, individual student habits are assumed to collectively translate into group routines; routines that are used to deliver a group presentation in each workshop. Student presentations serve as a primary interacting vehicle through which feedback is received. Repeated interaction enables groups and therefore individuals to alter their routines and habits of thought. Through means of assessment individual habits are ultimately differentially selected due to the nature of positive or negative feedback received concerning the group's performance.

The process begins with each group making decisions regarding the *content* and *context* (C/C) of their presentation, the *persons* and forms of *technology* (P/T) that will facilitate/deliver the presentation. In doing so, irrespective of their intentions, an image of their group based on its projected *identity* (I) is also offered for consumption. When taken together, these elements represent the nature of interaction through which the group's ongoing fitness will be determined. Next, a process of peer assessment (i.e. Peer$_1$, Peer$_2$, Peer$_3$, etc) occurs through which each group receives feedback and assessment as to their success or otherwise. There is an explicit focus upon content and context, with each element graded from 0 to 100%.

Students are required to specify what they liked and disliked about each performance. Within their assessment there is of course consideration given to the projected identity of the group through its choice of specific technologies (or the delivery processes) and the persons who have been physically present during the performance. Therefore, peer assessment acts as a selection mechanism, the outcome of which is a summative-based assessment (or a grading) and a formative assessment through which valuable written feedback is generated.

Thus, the group's interacting elements are continuously subjected to the evolutionary process of *variation*, *selection*, and *retention* (VSR). Post performance, each group must find a balance between the *freedom* (F.) to recombine their interacting elements and maintain the *discipline* (D.) to adhere to the workshop timetable and the perceived requirements of their audience. In actual fact, the process is more involved. At this point in time the nature of change occurring within and across all elements of the learning environment has not been discussed. This discussion will occur in Chapter 6. For now let us summarise the nature and proposed value of the reasonable adventurer.

Finding a Port in a Stormy Sea

Why should we spend so much time contemplating the development of a particular type of graduate? In Figure 4.3 below, a suggested life course for a typical EE student is contemplated. The timeline indicates a student commencing EE studies, graduating and then being free to act in an enterprising manner post-graduation. I have proposed that through organising curriculum development around an intermediate step (such as the reasonable adventurer) a higher degree of focus can be applied to *what* and *how* students could and should learn.

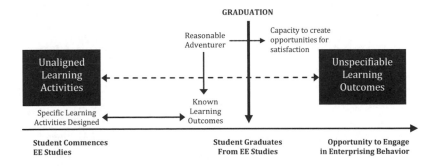

Figure 4.3   Suggested life course of a typical EE student

By placing a definite and attainable outcome for my EE students to work towards I am rewarded by knowing with much clarity what learning outcomes are appropriate. As a consequence, I am able to fit various types of learning activities, in which participation will enable the obtainment of the learning outcomes. Assuming that I am able to accurately assess the performance of my students, constructive alignment[14] is highly likely. Let's consider the alternative process illustrated in Figure 4.3. If you accept that we cannot know with any great certainty what forms of enterprise our students might engage in post-graduation, how do we know specifically what they need to learn? Should EE be reduced to technique and process? Can we guarantee the future value of knowledge gained today vis-à-vis the requirements of our students in their enterprising moments in the as yet unknown future? To the extent that we cannot know fully in advance what specific knowledge will be required we cannot know which specific learning activities would be most appropriate. Clearly this is not a desirable situation. Thus, the logic of an intermediate step emerges.

Let me provide you with an illustrative example. I see my students as possibly following four enterprising pathways. I describe the process leading towards each pathway as *stepping-up*[15] from their current place in life. First, my students might develop an enterprising career as a *worker* in an organisation not owned by them. Second, they could engage in some form of social entrepreneurship, acting essentially as a *servant* to society. Third, they could be a *saviour* to existing entrepreneurs by purchasing an existing business. Fourth, they could engage in start-up activities to be the *creator* of a new enterprise. I see all four pathways as being reconcilable with the need to ensure an intermediate step is presented to each EE student. A step that enables student choice as to what they wish to experience vis-à-vis their expected life journey. Thus, for me personally, the reasonable adventurer works well and fits in with my teaching philosophy. The real question then, is what position will you take in this debate?

DEVELOPING YOUR STUDENTS' ENTERPRISE SKILLS?

There are several critical questions you must consider in developing a curriculum for EE. First, *exactly* what do *your* students need to learn, and how can you facilitate this process of learning? This question will be repeatedly offered for your consideration throughout this book, because it truly matters. To give insufficient consideration to this question is to fail in your fundamental responsibility as an educator. Putting aside the challenge that you may be instructed by more senior colleagues as to what or how you should teach, let us consider this fundamental responsibility. A responsibility that is as complex as it is exciting.

Take a moment to step out of the EE world and take a wander into our particular corner of the education landscape. I would say that our corner is (or should be) tethered to all forms of experiential education. Increasingly, I am drawn to the work of Colin Beard,[16] which allows us all to move beyond the previous exemplary works in this area.[17] Beard has developed a unique focus on the outer world of the learner, the sensory interface of the learner and the inner world of the learner. From this perspective, we as educators are invited to consider the *places* where learning occurs. To ask what will our learners actually be *doing* when learning? To develop an interest in how they will *experience* their learning. To account for the nature of *emotional* engagement related to their learning. To consider what our learners need to know, and finally to ask how our learners can be encouraged to change.

We can simplify this challenge into the process of constructive alignment. Asking ourselves on behalf of our learners, what do they need to learn? What types of learning activities would best enable such learning to occur? Lastly, what forms of assessment would best enable us to determine their progress in obtaining the desired learning outcomes? However, as useful as this process is, it doesn't explicitly draw our attention into the outer, sensory and inner worlds of our students. A journey we must undertake to coherently explain how our learners learn.

Don't be daunted by this task, as complex as it may seem, it is achievable by us all. It is actually what we are paid to do unfortunately, the scholarship of teaching is increasingly diluted by the nature of how learning institutions function in the 21ˢᵗ century. Thus, your challenge is to rise above the acceptance of falling teaching standards and excel in your chosen profession so that your students can be guided in their studies. To do so, you need to understand how your students learn more so than you understand what they need to learn.

NOTES

1. See Jones (2007).
2. See Gibb (2002) to understand the full nature of the transformational role afforded to EE.
3. See Mahoney (2003).
4. See Hodgson (2001: 109) if you are not familiar with evolutionary processes, especially those that combine Lamarckian and Darwinian ideas.
5. See Heath (1964).
6. See Baxter-Magolda (2004).
7. See Baxter-Magolda (1998: 143).
8. See Dewey (1922).
9. See Whitehead (1929).

10. See Hodgson (2001).
11. See Gould (2002: 354).
12. See Hull (2001).
13. See Hodgson (2001: 109).
14. See Biggs (2003) to fully understand the importance of the notion of constructive alignment.
15. See http://www.step--up.com for an overview of the step--up pathways.
16. See Beard and Wilson (2002) to develop a sense of what is possible when we place the student's learning within the context of experiential learning.
17. See Boud, Keogh and Walker (1985).

5.   Student Diversity

There can be little doubt that as educators we are confronted with an ever-increasing level of student diversity within the higher education sector.[1] Within this chapter, I will argue that this provides educators with a unique opportunity to enhance the learning outcomes of our students. Building upon past research that highlights the relationship between increased superior learning outcomes from exposure to higher levels of student diversity,[2] this chapter aims to explain how to identify and use student diversity in a manner that enhances the development of enterprising skills. Essentially, the *elephant in the room* is revealed and asked to step forward and contribute, rather than remain silent (and hidden) away in the darkened corners of our classrooms.

Thus, this chapter challenges current approaches to defining the context and process of entrepreneurship education. The arguments presented here reflect a desire to bring to life (and celebrate) the ever-present diversity found within our classrooms. Any such attempt to advance this issue explicitly heightens a focus upon our efforts as educators, our students' efforts as learners, and our various teaching methods that bridge both parties. The following discussion is premised upon the notion that whilst students can learn as individuals, interaction with others has the potential to greatly advance learning outcomes, especially when the others collectively contribute to a heterogeneous learning environment.

As will be discussed shortly, the IE Survey provides some interesting insights into the psyche of EE educators. Whilst some see diversity as a non-issue, others argue that we should accept its presence but assure our students it is not a limiting factor to their aspirations. Alternatively, other respondents argue that accepting student diversity in our classrooms requires of educators the development of teaching methods that accommodate student diversity. I will not address these viewpoints directly. The focus of this chapter is to explain how to identify and exploit student diversity in EE. After these two challenges have been addressed, we will again return to the viewpoints of the IE Survey respondents. Then, as in preceding chapters you will have the opportunity to reflect upon your own position. Let us proceed first with the issue of how to identify student diversity in our classrooms.

The nature of our students' learning

IDENTIFYING STUDENT DIVERSITY

To measure any level of diversity, we must have dimensions of diversity. As recently discussed elsewhere,[3] student diversity can be conceived to be more than a construct related to social and ethnic origins. I have developed an index of student similarity to identify a level of diversity within a single class (and therefore also between classes). Adapted from Pianka's ecological Community Similarity Index,[4] the Student Similarity Index is simply expressed as X/N, where X is the number of student traits (or dimensions) common to each pair of students and N is the total number of student traits.

Eight dimensions have been adopted related to the students' background (i.e. age, origin and area of study), the current situation of the students (i.e. work commitments, effort committed to study and personal aspirations) and the students' approach to learning (i.e. learning style and learning personality). Let us consider how this method of identification can be operationalised. Using data from four enterprise units I taught at UTAS in 2009, it can be observed in Table 5.1 below that *within* each class student similarity ranges from 43.04% to 59.61%.

Table 5.1   Student diversity within four UTAS enterprise units

		BMA213	BMA787	BAA510	BMA204
		Statistics			
N	Valid	120	78	190	2278
	Missing	2173	2215	2103	15
Mean		.4304	.4655	.5961	.4612
Std error of mean		.01783	.01952	.01088	.00377
Std deviation		.19529	.17236	.15003	.17987
Variance		.038	.030	.023	.032
Range		.88	.75	.75	1.00
Minimum		.00	.13	.25	.00
Maximum		.88	.88	1.00	1.00

The relatively low levels of similarity indicate the degree to which students in each unit differ with their responses across the eight dimensions used. What is not directly apparent is on what basis the student diversity within each unit actually differs. Why might we like to know how the students in different units differ? Well, do you think that you can operate as an educator in the same manner regardless of the student cohort you encounter? Intuitively, good educators adjust aspects of their performance to align their contribution to the needs of their learners. However, should we rely upon *automatic* intuition, or should something else a little more deliberate guide this process of adjustment? In Figure 5.1 below we are able to observe the nature of student diversity *across* four units.

Canonical Discriminant Functions

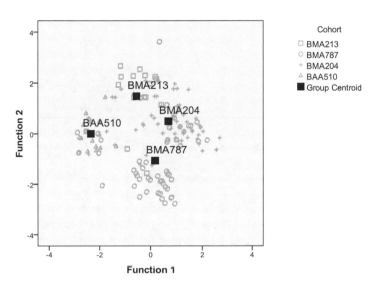

Figure 5.1   Student diversity across four UTAS enterprise units

A useful method of analysis to tease out *how* the enterprise units might differ in respect of student diversity is canonical discriminant analysis. Using the individual units as a dependent categorical variable, we can test the relationship between each unit and eight independent variables, or dimensions (noted previously as age, origin, area of study, work commitments, effort committed to study, personal aspirations, learning style and learning personality).

The results reveal that, statistically, there is a highly significant difference between the examined units across a combination (of discriminant functions) of the following variables: work commitments, maturity (or age), student type (their origin) and learning style. These variables (illustrated in the structure matrix in Table 5.2) provide insights into the varied composition of each unit that give rise to specific and unique levels of student diversity in each unit.

The nature of our students' learning

Table 5.2   Structure matrix

	Function		
	1	2	3
Work commitments	.787*	−.172	.496
Effort	.201*	−.046	−.038
Mature	.580	.603*	−.252
StudentTYPE	−.500	.508*	.384
Approach	−.074	−.142*	.125
LearningSTYLE	.002	.090	.416*
Faculty	.097	.161	−.194*
Aspirations	.081	.120	−.120*

Notes:
Pooled within-groups correlations between discriminating variables and standardised canonical discriminant functions.
Variables ordered by absolute size of correlation within function.
*   Largest absolute correlation between each variable and any discriminant function.

Whilst much of the variance of the model is explained by the first two discriminant functions (see Table 5.3 and Table 5.4 below), the Wilks' lambda values indicate that all four variables are useful within the model. The association between the discriminant scores and the units is strongly correlated, as evidenced by the level of the eigenvalues. The incorporated chi-square statistic tests the extent that the means of the functions used are equal across the units investigated. The small significance value indicates that the discriminant function does better than chance at separating the units.

So what does this tell us? Well, the educator is able to quantify the nature and degree of student diversity within and between units. Essentially, the characteristics of the elephant in the room are revealed. A real benefit from this process is that the students can be informed about the nature of diversity in the room. As previously discussed, the very nature of the reasonable adventurer is premised upon a greater awareness of self and those interacted with. In the next chapter, the full consequences of such awareness will be discussed in finer detail. It is acknowledged that the eight dimensions of student diversity employed do not represent an exhaustive list of dimensions. Indeed, many of the dimensions could be further broken down (e.g. international students). However, the dimensions do allow for insightful consideration of how student diversity actually occurs within and across units.

Table 5.3 Eigenvalues

		Eigenvalues		
Function	Eigenvalue	% of Variance	Cumulative %	Canonical correlation
1	.946[a]	51.8	51.8	.697
2	.723[a]	39.6	91.4	.648
3	.158[a]	8.6	100.0	.369

Note:
a. First three canonical discriminant functions were used in the analysis.

Table 5.4 Wilks' lambda

		Wilk's Lambda		
Test of function(s)	Wilk's Lambda	Chi-square	df	Sig.
1 through 3	.258	419.161	24	.000
2 through 3	.501	213.364	14	.000
3	.864	45.245	6	.000

STUDENT DIVERSITY ACROSS UNITS

If we focus upon the four dimensions highlighted through the use of canonical discriminant analysis, we can observe in Table 5.5 several specific differences. The first dimension was that of work status. What can be observed is that in BAA510, 80% of students work in excess of 40 hours per week, whereas in BMA787, only 3.7% of students work in excess of 40 hours. Whilst this difference is explainable by the composition of international students within these two post-graduate units, it nevertheless has implications for the time students can devote to their learning. Likewise, the difference between BMA213 and BMA204 in terms of the composition of international students is considerable, 6.3% to 67.7% respectively. Both undergraduate units are targeted at second year students. Clearly, from one semester to the next, it may not be wise to assume that the dynamics in our classrooms are predictable. Likewise, significant differences will likely exist between the learning style preferences between classes, as indicated in Table 5.5 below.

The nature of our students' learning

Table 5.5   Selected dimensions of student diversity

	Work Status		Mature	Student Type	Learning Style
	>40hrs	Don't Work	>25	International Students	Listening & Talking
BMA213	6.3%	12.5%	31.3%	6.3%	12.5%
BMA787	3.7%	42.6%	68.5%	85.2%	35.2%
BAA510	80.0%	0.0%	95.0%	0.0%	40.0%
BMA204	4.6%	29.2%	12.3%	67.7%	35.4%

The implications for the educator are clear and not trivial. First, despite the fact that a particular approach has worked previously, it should not be assumed that the next opportunity to use such an approach will occur in identical circumstances. Indeed, I have witnessed the dimensions of student diversity shift radically between semesters. Clearly, differing enterprising aspirations and capacities/willingness to learn create challenges to developing convergent learning outcomes. That is, realistically, achieving similar learning outcomes across a collective with degrees of similarity of less than 50% is not possible. To assume this is possible is to ignore the elephant in the room.

You may be asking yourself now how can we possibly entertain accommodating such variance in the learning outcomes of our students? It is a little scary (in this day and age of quality assurance) to contemplate actually deliberately teaching in a manner that incorporates the reality of ever-present student diversity. Where the outcomes our students achieve are reflective of their differences across a range of dimensions that extend well beyond assumed cognitive differences.

I argue that the key to incorporating student diversity into our approach to teaching enterprise is to assess the *process* where possible, and not merely default to assessing the more traditional material artefacts of student learning. The notion of explicitly assessing the process will be further discussed in detail in Chapter 9. Let us now consider this issue within the context of student diversity occurring *within* a unit.

STUDENT DIVERSITY WITHIN UNITS

Consistently observing low levels of student similarity in our classes requires the dedicated enterprise educator to accept diversity as an integral aspect of the learning environment. I say *accept* from a perspective of positively using diversity to advance the opportunities for student learning. Previously, I have discussed the value of student reflection. Now we can extend the nature of such discussion to include the use of forms of meta-reflection through which the students take stock of how their thoughts, feelings and attitudes differ and/or are similar to their fellow students. This process of reflection is referred to here as group sense making, a process adapted from the domain of nursing education.[5]

The aim of the group sense-making process is to lift the lid on hidden differences and similarities that exist between students. Further, to allow any such differences and similarities to be known and used by the students to aid their learning. The process is designed to allow a deeper appreciation of one's personal feelings, but also appreciation of the feelings of other students in the class. The process is completed through four phases, which are proceeded by a situation statement, developed by the educator to provide a provocative focus around a particular issue. The four phases are as follows:

Phase 1

The students identify and record their personal feelings related to the situation statement. It is quite likely they may experience more than one feeling. Conflicting feelings and/or those feelings that change over time should be noted. It is important that they don't only note the assumed or described feelings, but also their actual feelings.

Phase 2

The students (as a group) attempt to make sense of the context in the situation statement, now using the perspectives of all involved group members. They use the identified feelings to develop a sense of meaning vis-à-vis the collective feelings reported by the group members. This analysis may incorporate an exploration of personal beliefs, dispositions, experiences and attitudes. They typically conclude by speculating as to the meaning others attributed to the situation based on the collective feelings reported.

Phase 3

Each individual student now attempts to validate their analysis of the situation by asking for feedback from other (external) participants, peers etc. In other words, the meaning attributed to the situation is confirmed (or disconfirmed) with reference to the ideas and perspectives of others and/or through personal reflection of their own personal experiences.

Phase 4

Each student indicates how reflection on the situation has influenced their approach and/or perspective to this specific issue. Any possible shift in values, beliefs and/or attitudes is also noted. The following comments are representative comments of students currently using both forms of reflective practice.

> The use of reflective learning has allowed for a heightened personal learning experience. It requires a more deep level of thought on self which makes the student more aware of how they are going and to look both more critically at the work completed as well as the positive achievement that has been had not in terms of marks but in a more personal way. (student comment no. 1)

> From my experience the group sense making helped me to broaden my view of the subject. For example, after reading the other members of my group's phase one I had other perspectives I had not thought of but still either agreed with or could understand where they were coming from. Also, if what I had written in my phase one was echoed by other members of my group, then I felt more confident that I was on the right track. I think the reflections also give the educator valuable insight into how the student is feeling and how they perceive their learning to be progressing. (student comment no. 2)

> I would say that the reflection exercises allowed me to see from a different perspective my beliefs and attitudes. In relation to personal learning, this allowed me to easily criticize my learning patterns, and realize what needs to be fixed. In relation to group behavior, it allowed me to see what others might think of my behavior. (student comment no. 3)

> The reflection journals helped me consolidate what my strengths and areas for improvement were in reference to the course. The group situation statements were beneficial. They helped us to work in groups and effectively convey our feelings and ideas whilst enabling our entrepreneurial capacity. (student comment no. 4)

> After those experiential learning exercises I gained great insight into myself from the group sense making process. I have found it to be insightful, clarifying and helpful for me personally. I imagine that it will not only be me who benefits from this reflection exercise, but the lecturer will also gain a greater understanding of my personal learning outcomes than if I didn't complete the reflection. (student comment no. 5)

What is evident from the above comments is the recognition by the students of how their exposure to student diversity has benefited them. I would also add that it is of great benefit to me as an educator to have a ringside seat throughout this process as well. Rather than merely allowing the student to reflect, the provision of group sense making allows multiple perspectives to be shared by students and the educator. Put simply, it is the diversity within the student cohort that is used to increase individual student learning outcomes. It is central to the genuine possibility of student transformation. The key issue being the degree to which students are able to recognise such diversity and how it impacts their development in the learning environment. Interestingly, this issue of reflection did not surface in the IE Survey.

CONSIDERING DIVERSITY IN A GLOBAL CONTEXT

Not one respondent to the IE Survey noted the importance of student reflection when asked to discuss the implications to EE of student diversity. There were three schools of thought present in the responses. First, a minority stated that there are no teaching and learning implications for EE from the presence of student diversity. Such views appeared to be premised on the assumption that any such diversity was common to areas of teaching and learning and therefore EE educators should not be overly concerned. The second espoused a view that seemed to suggest that whilst they recognised the presence of diversity, the integrity of the curriculum can't be reshaped to accommodate the specific needs of all students. This second type of response scares me more than the first type. It is as if the elephant has been pushed back into the darkest corners of classrooms. What a waste of an opportunity to bring reality and intellectual curiosity into our learners' lives. What a waste of our efforts as educators to become intimately associated with the things that matter and truly make a difference in our classrooms.

However, the third and most dominant type of response to the IE Survey restores my confidence that EE educators can see the benefits of exploiting ever-present student diversity. Monica Kreuger, President of Global Infobrokers in Canada, notes that entrepreneurs are different from each other, therefore, as educators we should be encouraging diversity and setting up our learning environment to accommodate diverse needs. Professor Luke Pittaway of Georgia Southern University in Savannah argues that the main implication is to ensure a range of different learning styles are catered for, and that courses are clear about their objectives and that we keep in mind the issue of diversity when designing courses. Gary Hancock at the University of Adelaide in Australia also felt that exploiting student diversity represents a great opportunity to have students learn from each other, essentially allowing us as educators to tap into the reality of the world of entrepreneurship.

Another issue raised in the IE Survey related to the nature of student diversity. Dr Kirk Heriot of Columbus State University in Georgia noted with caution that you cannot ignore the fact that our students may work full time or over 30 hours per week. It is a big distraction, especially if they are working and taking three or four classes per week. The Student Similarity Index discussed earlier accounts for such difference and thus is argued to assist the educators and learners to appreciate just how the students differ. It is clearly not enough to accept that student diversity exists. To paraphrase the American ecologist Paul Sears,[6] when the educator enters the learning environment, he or she sees not merely what is there, but what is happening there. That is, we can gather data about our students and decipher the manner in which our students interact in their various learning environments. I say *various* because we should not assume that our students view their learning environs in the same light as the students immediately around them. This is the *essence* of student diversity, the fact that diversity as an input relates directly to differences experienced throughout the learning process by our individual students. So, the challenge of celebrating student diversity awaits you.

MAKING THE ELEPHANT YOUR FRIEND

The reality is that if you are serious about improving your students' learning outcomes, student diversity is an issue that you must willingly confront. If you can accept that you are unlikely to fully satisfy the *individual* learning needs of students within any particular cohort, then you must develop an approach to this issue. Again, I stress any such approach should be less about accommodating diversity, and more related to celebrating diversity. Let's consider a range of issues that may help you to develop a successful approach to this issue.

The first issue that should be tackled is your own knowledge and understanding of student diversity. To what extent have you researched this issue within the context of your teaching? To what extent do you naturally feel disposed towards making adjustments in the delivery of your teaching style to accommodate different styles and modes of learning? Clearly, the gist of this discussion is about all parties being flexible in the way they view the other. That to do so opens up another frontier upon which deeper learning can occur.

The second issue relates the options you avail your students with regards to their progression in your subject. A famous football coach[7] in Australia once said you can fry a sausage, you can BBQ a sausage and you can grill a sausage but at the end of the day it's still a sausage. The logic of this quote can be reversed to suit our purposes. Our students should be able to choose from a number of different learning methods within the one subject and still be deemed as having completed the subject. Sounds a little farfetched? My students are always given an open choice as to how they would like to complete their assignments. Whereas one student might like to submit a written assignment another might like to submit the same assignment in the form of a website, or an audio file, or face-to-face or via a telephone conversation, or through using a pitch-style presentation. The issue is not what format is most appropriate, but rather are the students able to demonstrate their learning vis-à-vis the required learning outcomes? In my context there is an emphasis on assessing their understanding or ability to complete a process. I am less concerned with the manner in which they demonstrate their learning than I am that they demonstrate their learning.

The third issue relates to whether you also have talking elephants in the room. I advocate employing a Student Similarity Index during the first class of the term/semester. It is useful for us as educators to know what degree of diversity exists, and it is really important for the students to also understand this as well. When EE students know that their style of approach, their aspirations and life circumstances are accepted in the learning environment they are freed from any concerns related to conforming to the norm. They are free to be themselves and approach their studies in a manner that maximises their progression given the context of their life.

The fourth issue relates to you. Are you willing to trust yourself to operate in an environment where expressed diversity leads to divergent learning outcomes? An environment within which the preferences of individual students rule over the hope that all students might end up experiencing a similar learning outcome. This issue again feeds back into the nature of the dialogic relationships you hold with your peers.

In summary, this chapter has argued the case for identifying, measuring and leveraging student diversity to increase the individual (and therefore collective) learning outcomes of students studying EE. The proposition is that it is through the *modification of thought* that students can truly navigate the challenging landscape that is EE.

NOTES

1. See Biggs (2003) for confirmation of the presence of student diversity and its increasing prominence.
2. See Gurin (1999) for his seminal report on the positive impacts of having student diversity as a factor in our students' learning.
3. See Jones (2010b).
4. See Pianka's (1973) index, which is simply X/N, where X is the number of sub-populations common to two towns and N is the total number of sub-populations occurring in either; thus community similarity equals 1 when two towns are identical, and 0 when they share no sub-populations.
5. See Hart et al. (1998) for their unique development of a group reflective process to better equip nursing graduates for the emotional challenges of nursing on a ward.

6.   See Sears (1980).
7.   Allan Jeans, Hawthorn Football Coach, 1981–1987, 1989–1990.

6.   The Learning Environment

Having contemplated the nature of student diversity occurring naturally in our learning environments, and contemplating its worth, let us now consider in more detail the dynamics of the learning environment. Specifically, let us pause to reflect upon the elements that interact so as to enable learning to occur. It has been five years since I contemplated this issue.[1] On that first occasion, to considerable mixed reaction,[2] I pondered the extent to which students could be co-architects of the learning environments they experience. In this chapter I would like to revisit the importance of such musings and to challenge you to pause and consider which elements in your learning environments interact so as to determine the nature of learning outcomes achieved.

In doing so, I challenge you to be open to consideration of abstract notions of time and space. To remove yourself from the sole position of creator, and to imagine the possibility of your students performing the role of co-creator of the learning environments they encounter. I argue that to do so is to adopt a truly learner-centred approach to teaching and learning. An approach whereby our students' learning develops simultaneously as the learning environments they encounter are co-created. This foray into such an abstract discussion is not without some specific caveats.

ESSENTIAL GROUND RULES

First, this chapter employs an explicit evolutionary approach to highlight suggested causal processes and the nature of change in both the students and the learning environments they encounter. Second, and as noted previously, it has been argued[3] that for students to be engaged in a deeper process of learning, processes related to learning objectives, learning activities and assessment must be aligned. Importantly, this process of constructive alignment should also accommodate criterion-referenced assessment[4] as opposed to the more traditional norm-referenced assessment. Third, acceptance of the first two caveats opens the doorway for inclusion for an additional role for students. A role that sees student cohorts change from being separated by time, but perhaps not process, to cohorts joined in time and definitely process. To summarise the nature and parameters of this discussion, let us isolate our focus through the use of the following syllogism:

> The use of learner-centred teaching and learning pedagogies that incorporate criterion-based assessment will advance student learning outcomes.
>
> Criterion-based assessment processes used repeatedly enable students to understand their performance at a given point in time and provide guidance for individual and group advancement over time against specific curriculum objectives, therefore...
>
> Over time, a process of continual adjustment to learning objectives, learning activities and assessment procedures will be required to cater for improved student learning and dynamic student/learning environment interaction within and between learning cohorts.

Therefore, and with specific reference to the above syllogism, this chapter proceeds based upon several premises. First, providing increased freedom to students through a learner-centred approach is expected to increase the range of interaction possibilities between the students and their learning environments. Second, as educators, we must accept that it is not possible to create the perfect learning environment in advance of such unknown interaction. Third, as a result of the first two premises, it is useful to accept that the process of curriculum design quite likely represents a process that has no obvious starting or end point, and that it does not need one.

Whilst such ideas may seem logical as regards the process of genetic and social change that unfolds in our everyday life,[5] they nevertheless challenge the traditional legitimacy of the educator to assume sole responsibility for curriculum design and delivery. Indeed, this is the central argument outlined in this chapter. An argument that suggests the process of constructive alignment in the presence of repeated criterion-referenced assessment will most likely be interfered with by student advancement within and between cohorts. The extent to which such interference is positive or negative depends upon the role we ascribe to our students. Thus, this discussion represents a departure from the basic assumption that each cohort of students from one year to the next experiences a similar starting point and is subject to a (relatively) consistent experience of education. Let me share with you some observations of my students, and the role I recognise them contributing to the co-creation of the learning environments I oversee.

THE UTAS LEARNING ENVIRONMENT

Since 2002, EE has been offered to students at UTAS. During this time, I argue that EE has offered students a less traditional (within the context of UTAS) way to learn. The learner-centred approach discussed in Chapter 1 has evolved significantly since 2002, with the curriculum co-developed through frequent lecturer/student consultation. Fundamental to this approach has been a learner-centred approach designed to meet the requirements of EE.[6]

To recap, students are encouraged to learn in their here and now[7] and to develop many differing interpretations of the required learning topics. A critical determinate of the learning process has been the use of various forms of continuous student reflection related to the repeated learning tasks that occur between fortnightly workshops. As previously noted, the purpose of the learning activities developed and continually refined is to accelerate the 'process of changing the behaviour patterns ... [of the students] ... using behaviour in the broad sense to include thinking and feeling as well as overt action'.[8] Again, there are two specific aims of the programme. One relates to assisting students capable of making the journey from student to graduate entrepreneur to do so and the other (more general) aim relates to helping the students develop the attributes of a reasonable adventurer.

Ever-increasing degrees of freedom have been provided to the students regarding how they explore, explain and approach their learning tasks. The students' interactions with the learning environment and their contribution of artefacts (e.g. example, presentation formats) that have been carried forward have had a profound influence on the development of subsequent curriculums. The next section introduces an evolutionary model (see Figure 6.1) that helps to explain how such influence is thought to occur, before the implications of the model are considered in the concluding sections. Unfortunately, not all big ideas are reducible to a simple schema, and the ideas related to Figure 6.1 are typically quite challenging.

Niche Construction

The process illustrated in Figure 6.1 is an adaptation of Odling-Smee, Laland and Feldman's niche construction process.[9] In championing the neglected process of niche construction, they bring to life the previous work of Lewontin.[10] Lewontin sought to refute the assertion that an organism proposes (a set of predefined) solutions to the problems it encounters in its environment, and that the environment then efficiently rewards or punishes those solutions that prove beneficial or injurious to the organism. For Lewontin, any explanation of the process of adaptive change must cater for the ongoing reciprocal interaction between the organism, its generative mechanism and the environment. He asserted that organisms determine relevance, alter their external world and transduce physical signals from their external environment. Essentially, rather than merely being on the receiving end of natural selection, organisms both make and are made as a consequence of interaction with their environment.

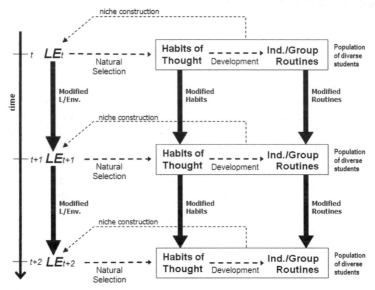

Figure 6.1   The proposed causal pathways of niche construction

Extending this way of thinking, Odling-Smee, Laland and Feldman again cast doubt on the conventional view that organisms adapt to their environment, but environments do not adapt to their organisms. Let us consider the educational implications. A conventional view would likely assume that student interaction within a particular learning environment would result in the sorting of students by specific (learning) traits as ordered by the assessment procedures they encounter. Further, that whilst some students may improve throughout the process, the structure of the learning environment would remain essentially unaltered through such interaction. It is highly likely that such a process could occur through the application of a lecturer-centred approach complete with the use of norm-reference assessment procedures. This is not what is being suggested here; let us return to Figure 6.1.

In Figure 6.1, it is assumed that both change internal to the student (i.e. their habits of thought) and external change (or, their phenotypic expression) are possible due to interaction with a learning environment (LE). The process begins with the interaction between a student as an individual and as a group member within the learning environment (LE_t). To begin with, each student and his or her group will engage in various learning activities, which will be assessed using both summative and formative feedback. During this process of assessment, the fitness of the routines used individually by each student and by his or her group will be selected either for or against. Such routines represent the mechanisms responsible for phenotypic expression (e.g. the content and context of the student's/group's performance and associated identity projected for consumption).

Consequently, each student's habits of thought[11] are subject to differential selection (for or against) on the basis of their contribution to the phenotypic expression of the individual or group. Then, a combination of freedom and reflection provide the means through which the group (and therefore individuals) may alter behaviours via a shift in their collective and separate habits of thought. This process of group and individual change is facilitated in the first instance by the summative information received (their grading) and then by the formative information that relates to both negative and positive aspects of the group's/individual's performance. So it is these various forms of assessment that act as selection mechanisms. The assumption, that without an explicit form of selection operating, a process of continuous improvement is not possible.

The practice of generating both summative and formative assessment is important to ensure two important functions are performed. First, the summative feedback provides an indication of the immediate fitness of the group's/individual's performance vis-à-vis the various performance criteria at a particular moment in time. Second, the formative feedback provides feedback through which future change is possible. John Biggs[12] notes that the 'difference between them is that at some point the judgement has to be final'. The other factor that influences the composition of the interacting elements is that of the internally held perceptions within the group that may be altered to produce many different outcomes.

Therefore, three forms of inheritance are possible and likely throughout this process. First, the students' habits of thought (derived from their habits of life) are subject to revision as they determine what mental capabilities will best assist their progress. Altered habits of thought are then inherited from one learning environment to the next (i.e. LE_t to LE_t+1) either via individual student behaviour or through their contribution to their group. Second, those aspects of the modified phenotypic expression (deemed to be favourable) and related to any changed habits of thought are inherited by the groups from one learning environment to the next (i.e. LE_t to LE_t+1). Third, and I would argue most interestingly, the behaviours of the individuals and their groups have the potential to alter the nature of future interaction between the learning environment and all entities to be assessed. Therefore, it is argued that niche construction provides a process within and through which students alter their learning environment in their time and space and/or at least place significant pressure on the learning environment within their time and space.

I have observed during my teaching that my students have been the continuous co-architects of an ever-changing learning environment. In its simplest form, such change has been determined through the changing perceptions of individuals that impact upon the process of peer assessment operating on and within group performances. Put simply, groups seemingly (as a collective) change their perceptions as to what satisfies the stated learning objectives contained within the process of criterion-based assessment. In doing so, the process of (natural) selection operating on both individuals and groups in the learning environment is altered. As a consequence, when students make profitable alterations to their individual and group habits of thought they do so locked in an inquisitive battle to find better solutions to the problems present in their learning environment. Many of the solutions they devise place substantial pressure on the nature of the learning activities used. This in turn places pressure on the structure of the learning activities used to stretch the students' capabilities. As such, the students have the ability to inherit a modified learning environment due to their direct and indirect influence on the essential elements of the learning environment.

CONTEMPLATING STUDENT-DRIVEN CHANGE

The above discussion challenges us all to reconcile our role as chief organiser of the learning environment. It is stimulating to reflect upon an ever-changing learning environment that is both demanding of students and also shaped by the needs and behaviour of students. However, contemplating such a process does not come without cost. The existence of such a process would logically place stress on any desire to achieve constructive alignment of learning objectives, learning activities and assessment procedures. Let us take a moment to play this issue forward a little.

Initially, we would seem to be confronted by two contradictory processes in niche construction and constructive alignment. However, I argue that there really isn't a significant contradiction at all. One process moves a system towards a stable equilibrium (i.e. constructive alignment) and the other shifts a system continually towards a dynamic equilibrium (i.e. niche construction). So whilst there is the potential for compatibility, there is essentially a temporal inconsistency. As noted by Veblen,[13] 'institutions are products of the past process, are adapted to past circumstances, and are therefore never in full accord with the requirements of the present'. I would argue that this temporal inconsistency is always occurring due to the constant adjusting of inner relations (or habits of thought) to outer relations (or the learning environment) when our students are encouraged to learn in their here and now.

We can illustrate this process diagrammatically in Figure 6.2 to better explain the nature of these processes. Constructive alignment holds that our development of learning outcomes directly influences that nature of learning activities used to advance our students' learning. Further, that the development of particular forms of learning activities in turn influences the nature of the assessment procedures used to ascertain our students' learning outcomes. Therefore, one process continues to inform the other process as alignment between learning outcomes, learning activities and assessment procedures increasingly becomes synchronised. However, there is no explicit accommodation of a role for students in this process. In Figure 6.2, changes to the students' habits of thought are shown as also placing pressure on both the nature of learning activities used and the process of assessment used to measure student learning. As such, a mediating process between learning activities and assessment procedures is also shown. This indicates the iterative nature of the process that interrupts the simple linear relationship between the three elements. I argue that these relationships now better represent the actual interaction between the elements.

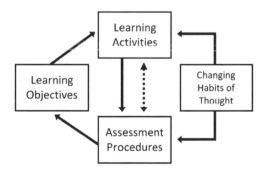

Figure 6.2   Combining niche construction and constructive alignment

I have observed that when using pure forms of learner-centred teaching complete with criterion-based assessment, another useful process emerges. Previously[14] I have explained a process of competitive bragging occurring through which the ideas and behaviours of each group are proudly put forward for consideration by fellow groups. As alternative ideas and techniques (e.g. the use of multi/social media) are revealed, *perceived* advantages are transferred across groups through imitation (and trial and error), resulting in mutations of assumed best practice. The entrepreneurial processes of reproduction and innovation flourish as students experiment and copy within the learning environment. Using assessment as a valuable guidance tool, the students are energised by the presence of their colleagues. Interestingly, I occasionally introduce assessment procedures that are more norm-referenced in design (or judgements concerning student versus student, or group versus group). Immediately, this has brought about the resumption of behaviours that could be best labelled competitive jockeying. Sadly, admiration is replaced with suspicion, openness gives way to secrecy and fair peer assessment is lost as students jockey for position.

Observing such radical change in classroom behaviour reminds me of how important my role is. Ensuring students have my support and guidance regardless of how many mistakes they make is critical to developing a progressive form of evolution in our learning environment. Kropotkin[15] argued that progressive evolution is built upon mutual aid, not survival of the fittest. His ageless ideas very much capture the spirit within which modified selection forces take shape in the learning environments I share with my students.

To summarise, I have argued that our students can perform the role of co-architect of the learning environments within which they learn. That the progressive development of our students can be explained with reference to a modified evolutionary process. From this perspective, it is the students' habits of thought that are altered to advance their ability to succeed in the learning environments. This process assumes that students develop the means to challenge their own 'assumptions about the nature, limits, and certainty of knowledge'.[16] Clearly, there is an assumption being made that the students are capable of constructing the meaning of their learning experiences. Thus, repeated reflective processes occurring within and between workshops give rise to knowing being associated with action,[17] resulting in upward (positive) pressure being placed on all elements of the learning environment. Pressure, that in the short term appears to threaten the potential attainment of a constructively aligned stable curriculum.

However, evolution is never that simple, there is no starting or end point. Indeed past work related to evolution and learning[18] suggests that the predicament that both the lecturer and the student face is like searching for a needle in a haystack. There is no optimal path to conduct such a search, only helpful voices in the dark that guide our search. For my students that voice has been frequent formative and summative feedback. For me, that voice has been regular feedback from the students related to all aspects of the learning environment they interact with. Disappointingly, the IE Survey shone little light onto the issue of students as co-architects of the learning environment.

THE IMPLICATIONS FOR EDUCATORS

The issue of student development occurring alongside the alteration of the learning environment drew little comment from the IE Survey. However, several educators noted interesting aspects of this nascent debate. Professor Ted Fuller at Lincoln University in the UK argues that we need to give agency to students where possible to develop the learning environment. David Gibson of Queens University in Belfast notes the importance of educators having to adapt and develop along with their learners' needs. Professor David Kirby of the British University in Egypt recognised the inherent opportunities for educators teaching entrepreneurship in ever-changing learning environments. He noted that we should encourage our students to find themselves, to question, to develop creative solutions to problems, to be pro-active etc. In other words, there is an opportunity to exploit the shifting sands of our environs to the advantage of all concerned.

Monica Kreuger, President of Global Infobrokers in Canada, argues that we should embrace the change, that we should use it to show how to adapt to change, that this is the reality of the entrepreneur, and that we can show that they have the ability to make change. Professor Colin Gray of the Open University senses that our aim should be to alter the students' experience as we progress in precisely this way. As Professor Andy Penaluna of the Swansea Metropolitan University in the UK asserts, our challenge as educators is to manage the incremental nature of such change, so that it can be observed and understood by the students. The recent research of Penaluna and his colleagues[19] demonstrates the reality of this challenge, noting that not all learning (and therefore change) will occur incrementally, as *aha* moments frequently disrupt the underlying process of learning. What is apparent from such opinions is the need for us to become students of our classroom dynamics. As educators we need to be able to see change occurring within and between students, we need to be able to take receipt of artefacts that evidence such change. For me personally, as explained in the previous chapter, I used student reflection to invite myself into this process. I frame my interventions in such a way as to positively intrude on my students' learning. We also use classroom discussions to act as a form of informal formative feedback from which the students and I can take measure of what is occurring in the classroom. In essence, we cannot lay claim to involvement with a process of education that has transformative potential if we can't explain how any such effect is possible. Veblen[20] famously stated:

> If any portion or class of society is sheltered from the action of the environment in any essential respect, that portion of the community, or that class, will adapt its views and its scheme of life more tardily to the altered general situation; it will in so far tend to retard the process of social transformation.

Clearly there is an onus upon us to ensure that we and our students recognise the nature of the *environmental action* occurring in our classrooms. To not do so would be to shelter our students from the forces that have the capacity to alter their habits of life in such a way as to facilitate readjustment to the shifting requirements of the day. The key issue at stake here is that processes of adjustment don't occur by accident. The extent to which educators and students understand the nature of interaction occurring provides the basis through which profitable change can occur. Let us now consider this issue as it might relate to you.

CONTEMPLATING YOUR LEARNING ENVIRONMENTS

How might the process of niche construction play out in your learning environments? A useful place to start is to consider the nature of assessment operating in your students' learning environments. Is assessment used frequently? Does assessment comprise both formative and summative components? Is a criterion-based approach used to encourage all students to strive for success vis-à-vis the learning outcomes? Is peer assessment used to enable students to assess each other? To the extent you have answered these questions positively, you are potentially operating in a similar assessment environment to me. To the extent you answered the questions in the negative; perhaps there are challenges in conceptualising a world within which your students are the co-architects of the learning environment.

Assessment acts as a form of selection, providing immediate guidance as to what works and what doesn't. The more frequently you assess your students' behaviour, the more opportunities they have to alter their habits of life. For example, my students are assessed every fortnightly workshop. They receive both summative and formative feedback through which their planning for the next period of time is shaped. In this respect, assessment is a critical factor in enabling the transformation of the students between workshops. It is not the intervention of the educator that matters; it is the introspection of the student that matters most. The students' food for thought is delivered from a regular diet of summative and formative feedback. In the absence of regular feedback, our students will be left hungry and denied the opportunity to adapt to the shifting requirements of their next challenge.

However, feedback is also critically important to the educator. How often do you receive regular, honest and frank feedback from your students? Is it more than once or twice a semester? In the absence of such feedback from our students we are guessing as to their needs. During the last few years I have regularly given my students a small slip of paper to complete after each workshop. With regards to the degree they felt engaged in the workshop, the students were asked to place a value on my facilitation of the workshop, ranging from zero cents to a dollar. The students were also asked to briefly explain their judgement. Thus, I was constantly in receipt of vital information as to what was working and what wasn't. I was able to measure my improvement across the semester as I sought to address their needs in real time. Most importantly, we became partners in a *contract to learn*, a contract that increased our capacity to understand and forgive each other. Such activities have the potential to increase the rate of change in our classrooms. They have the ability to bring a sharper focus as to the actual reason we find ourselves in a classroom. They have the capacity to increase our thinking about our thinking. The process of change need not be silent and invisible. It can be celebrated and used to advance the process of everyone's learning.

So, to recap, a useful way of supporting the process of niche construction is to gather regular informal and formal feedback. This process can serve as both an invitation and a means of legitimising both the role of students as change agents and the formation of any new habits of thought under consideration. A very simple way to proceed would be to ask students what aspects of the learning environment should be kept, added and/or removed so as to aid their learning. This process may provide access to very rich and insightful comments that could guide modifications to the learning environment with greater surety.

Why might it be necessary to get down into the trenches and fight alongside our students? Surely we hold sufficient power to instruct our students as to the requirements of their studies? I argue that the biggest value gain EE students make is the development of various forms of confidence. Confidence in who they are. Confidence in what skills they have developed. Confidence in their ability to interact with their peers. Confidence in their ideas. Confidence in their ability to communicate their dreams and visions. Confidence that extends to their ability to make sense of change in the world they live in, and confidence in their ability to bring about change in that same world. It is for these very reasons that we should become partners in the processes of learning. What lies beyond our classrooms will test the confidence of every student we graduate. The opportunities to develop and test the resilience of their confidence should occur frequently during their studies, not afterwards when they are truly alone. There are several issues related to the development and testing of such confidence that have not being discussed here. They deserve brief mention so as to ensure their future discussion elsewhere.

As we assist our students to understand themselves vis-à-vis their potential resilience and/or optimism, do we adequately prepare them for the realities of personal failure? To what extent do our students' studies allow them to come to grips with the potential challenges of depression, loneliness and a general capacity to comprehend the dark side of entrepreneurship? We do our students no favours in not acknowledging the personal challenges associated with seeking to bring about forms of social change and/or to be ultimately responsible for the stewardship of an enterprise in society. Appropriately, the next issue that will be discussed relates to the resource foundations upon which such confidence will be built.

NOTES

1. See Jones (2006b).
2. I received three reviews. One reviewer said, 'The literature and theory behind this paper will seem strange to educationalists, even though it deals with issues of importance in education'. Another reviewer said, 'This is an insightful and creative critique which argues for an adaptive, learner-centred re-interpretation of Biggs' (2003) framework of constructive alignment. In bringing in Lewontin's evolutionary ideas, it brings a broader systems perspective to this well-known framework and should be useful to higher education teachers and researchers, curriculum designers and academic developers. In particular, it recognises that in truly learner-centred environments, students co-create the learning environment that they experience. Some may find the paper controversial, but as such it is likely to make a welcome contribution to academic debate'. The last reviewer stated, 'The discussion of adult learning as niche construction in response to formative feedback was the most mechanistic, reductionist, behaviourist account I've read since the 60s and seems totally at odds with contemporary understandings of the complexities involved'.
3. See Biggs (2003).
4. For those not familiar with criterion reference assessment, rather than comparing students with each other, the focus is upon comparing individual students against a set of pre-determined learning objectives.
5. See Veblen (1925) for an enlightened discussion of the nature of social change in society.
6. As outlined by Gibb (2002) in his consistent argument that we must transfer responsibility of learning to the learner.
7. See Whitehead (1929).
8. See Tyler (1949: 5–6).
9. See Odling-Smee, Laland and Feldman (2003) for their wonderful resurrection of a concept that whilst discussed by Darwin himself, has remained largely neglected since.
10. See Lewontin (1983).
11. See Veblen (1925).
12. See Biggs (2003: 142).
13. See Veblen (1925: 191).
14. See Jones (2006b).

15. See Kropotkin (1902) to gain an alternative understanding of the process of evolution in which it is cooperation that underpins the progressive evolution of specific entities.
16. See Baxter-Magolda (2004: 16).
17. See King and Kitchener (1994).
18. See Hinton and Nowlan (1987) for their clever discussion of how imprecise, yet important the search process is to the process of evolution.
19. See Penaluna, Coates and Penaluna (2010) for a detailed discussion of the process of assessing and understanding creativity and learning.
20. See Veblen (1925: 193).

7.   The Resource Profile

It seems we are increasingly surrounded by incredible stories of EE students that have achieved overnight entrepreneurial success. Students whose entrepreneurial adventures are seemingly linked directly to their higher education studies. Such stories cut through the gloom of declining graduate opportunities to give hope, but is it false hope? I say by and large it is; I say we need to develop more humility regarding the potential ability of our graduates to engage in start-up activities upon (or before) graduation. I say we need to replace a focus on romantic notions of the role and importance of EE with a more practical account of the potential value of EE. To not do so is to perpetuate a myth that very few educators and/or students can live up to.

Sound a little negative? Do the sums, how many of your students graduate as owners of a business that will support their actual (or intended) lifestyle? To the extent that we do have some students that start up a successful business, can we definitely demonstrate this would not have been possible without their participation in EE at higher education? As previously noted, we are faced with the reality of the actual current rate of graduate entrepreneurship and the ontological nature of EE, as discussed in Chapter 3. I will argue in this chapter that it is our tendency as educators to over-emphasise the business context of enterprise that creates a headache for us. We cannot guarantee that every EE student will become an entrepreneur, but we should be able to guarantee every EE student an opportunity to develop enterprising skills and experience entrepreneurial behaviour. To further this discussion, the notion of the resource profile will be discussed and its proposed importance will be demonstrated across a range of contexts.

THE STUDENT RESOURCE PROFILE

Students with entrepreneurial intentions are not shielded from the realities of the world. Their medium- to long-term outcomes will be derived from the same success/failure factors as all other entrepreneurs. It is important that we never lose sight of this very important fact. To think otherwise is to provide false hope to our students. Once our students sit down to play in the real world, they will need the same level of skills as other entrepreneurs and will most likely be dealt the same degree of good luck and bad luck as everybody else.

Our challenge is to ensure they understand how to play the game, when to be bold and when to retreat. To achieve this level of understanding our students need to intimately appreciate what skills and resources they have. They also need to understand how to assess the potential application of any such skills and resources to a particular opportunity. I argue that we can advance the future entrepreneurial capacity of our students by highlighting the value (or otherwise) of their resource profile vis-à-vis a range of enterprise opportunities. Think of our skeletons. We rely upon them to provide structure to our bodies, to enable our muscles to work in a coordinated manner. But if we didn't have the ability to x-ray our bodies, how would we know everything was connected and in the right place? Developing an understanding of our resource profile is akin to x-raying our body. We get to audit our entrepreneurial capacity in relation to a particular idea. We get to understand what structures and systems are present through which the process of entrepreneurship can be attempted.

It is commonly accepted that for any opportunity an individual or group will hold a resource profile relative to that opportunity.[1] A resource profile can be thought to comprise human, financial and social capital. It is argued that what we know and who we know, combined with our ability to gain access and control of vital resources, go a long way to explaining our potential entrepreneurial success. Have you observed the fatal flaw in this seemingly obvious logic? Remember the opportunities our students pursue are not shielded from the realities of the world. Yet our students will almost certainly hold an inferior resource profile compared with other more seasoned entrepreneurs. Accepting this proposition requires of EE educators a capacity to be candid about when and how EE students should engage with entrepreneurial opportunities.

What is not being suggested is that our students by and large are too inexperienced to engage with entrepreneurial opportunities. In fact quite the opposite; I feel our students need to engage with as many entrepreneurial opportunities as possible. Let me explain my thinking in this regard. Too often our students are steered towards creating *in their minds* an idea to build a business plan around. An idea born from imagination of one's life, that typically has little hope of relating to a strong resource profile, and therefore an idea that may be essentially unachievable. It is very important to note that whilst a student may have a strong resource profile for one idea they may have a weak resource profile relative to another idea. My basic argument; resource profiles are more idea specific than people specific. So we potentially fail our students by letting them pursue the development of an idea to which they have insufficient resource profile potentiality. Essentially, a learning opportunity may be squandered when we allow their focus and energy to be directed to such unattainable ideas.

However, all is not lost; indeed recognition that such a reality exists creates endless opportunities for us as educators. Indeed, it has been the inspiration for my 4Cs approach whereby my students in every unit must *conceive* new value, they must *create* it, they must *capture* it and, most importantly, they must *critique* their efforts to do so. Adopting this approach has enabled the development of three quite distinct ways of developing awareness of each student's resource profile. Let us consider each of the three approaches.

Resource Profile Upsizing

Entrepreneurial events do not occur in isolation, they occur within social settings. Understanding the nature of social and human capital, how it is formed and used to facilitate entrepreneurial activity is of critical importance. It is vital the students appreciate that social and human capital is rarely developed in a deliberate manner. Take a moment to think about this. If you can't know in advance what entrepreneurial endeavours you will be engaged with, you surely can't know in advance who or what you will need to know to assist your efforts. Thus, social and human capitals are quite often latent assets that emerge to connect the dots as entrepreneurs act. So, how might we help our students to be capable of connecting the dots?

The 4Cs approach requires of the students an action-oriented approach to contemplating and then attempting some act of enterprise. In the first stage, students are encouraged to conceive some new form of value. Whilst some students may align their thinking to ideas to which they already have social and human capital, most don't. The challenge is to let the students' ideas stand, to not reveal a judgement as to the suitability of the idea vis-à-vis the student's likely resource profile. Then, with an idea on the drawing board the student must contemplate the conditions required to create and capture the expected value. Who do they need to know to access assumed vital resources? Who do they need to know to access assumed vital technical knowledge? What do they need to know to operationalise their assumed business model?

Answering these questions leads to a list of contacts, forms of knowledge and skills that must accompany the student in the event the idea was progressed. At this point in time the list can be shared across the classroom. To what extent can the student's resource profile be upsized through sharing this list of needs with the other students? Who do they (or I) know that would add value to another student's resource profile? What is evident from this process is that by allowing the student to live in a future moment of time, the actual resource-related realities of their idea have space to emerge. The gaps in their resource profile can be seen by the other students and possible assistance can be offered to increase the potential resource profile the student has.

Resource Profile Downsizing

The process of upsizing is potentially limited by actual coordination factors that prevent the development of a superior resource profile. Whilst we might know who would add value to any future collective resource profile, their actual input might not be possible. Therefore, whilst such an approach may potentially be useful, it may also in reality be more of a theoretical learning tool. An alternative approach is resource profile downsizing. Within this approach all four phases of the 4Cs approach can be employed against the reality of the world the students live in. The aim here is to immerse the students into smaller, more manageable challenges through which the entire cycle of conceive, create, capture and critique can be completed several times. Let us consider some examples.

Students operating in groups of six to eight are given an opportunity to run a restaurant for one sitting. They don't need to create a restaurant, they just need to run an existing one. Clearly a degree of the risk has been eliminated from the process, yet they must still conceive what type of value they believe they can create and ultimately capture. To chart the way forward, the most successful groups tend to step back and examine their collective *potential* resource profile. I say potential resource profile because until they move the idea from their minds to the reality of seeking paying customers, that is all it is. Having determined who is known and what expertise and other resources can be accessed, the various ideas of the group as to what type of event they will run tend to take shape.

Let us briefly consider the process of the less successful groups. They tended to be overwhelmed by the excitement of a concept or theme that at face value will be attractive to an as yet to be confirmed target market. Their efforts tend to be hijacked early in the piece by something other than the reality of their potential collective resource profile. It has been said that entrepreneurs are *dreamers who do*,[2] but I would argue that something very important exists between the dreaming and doing stages. It is not enough to simply dream it, there must also exist an ability to convert the dream into a reality. The students who build their dreams around the actual potential of their collective resource profile have a solid foundation for the value they conceive. Those that do not are essentially making a much larger investment in lady luck.

Throughout this process the students are acting entrepreneurially, attempting to create and capture new value. The process is real. It is not stage managed, it is not theoretical, and they can make a profit or incur a financial loss. Along the way they share their planning with the other groups in the fortnightly workshops; they receive encouragement and feedback from each other. Thus, they are able to critique the process as it unfolds. They are able to recover lost ground before it is too late. They are able to live the moment in slow motion. They will be surprised by lucky breaks and disappointed by others that let them down. But of most importance, they will be accountable to their planning when they serve either empty or full chairs in *their* restaurant.

Without doubt, this process is exacting upon the students, it tests their resilience, and it tests their commitment, their patience, their appreciation of each other and their ability to understand how they themselves have framed the terms of their success or failure. They make sense of their success or failure by auditing themselves with reference to how their potential resource profile measured up against their actual resource profile used in the challenge. Invariably, those groups that have understood and utilised their potential resource profile outperform those that have not. They demonstrate a capacity to call in favours, to gain access to resources at low or no cost. They use their social contacts to understand and attract a particular type of target market. They make profits from their first few customers, not the last few expected customers. But to my satisfaction, both types of groups can learn from the experience equally. The lesson as to why profits and/or a loss have been made can be equally discerned from the aftermath of each outcome. Again it is the value of student reflection that elevates the nature of the learning achieved through the internalisation of the process at the personal level. Let us now consider the third way of creating awareness of the students' resource profiles.

Resource Profile Fitting

What if we have a student determined to start a new business venture, or a curriculum requirement that students must complete a business plan in order to complete their studies? In both situations, the issue of their potential resource profile is of critical importance. I argue that in both cases the student be encouraged to fit their pre-existing resource profile to a specific type of business opportunity. Clearly it is important for each student to understand more than what they are passionate about. They need to also have a handle on who needs to be known relative to a particular idea. What forms of knowledge will be required to succeed in developing their idea? What resources must be accessed and/or controlled in order to succeed in the opportunity space?

The opportunity that exists here is to guide the students' selection of an entrepreneurial idea. The aim is not to deter their efforts but rather to help them to better align their efforts to avoid them becoming a *dreamer who doesn't*. Whilst we need our students to be acting entrepreneurially, we need such efforts to be as well directed as possible. It serves little purpose for our students to spend their time and effort on trying to make sense of an entrepreneurial idea to which they have little resource profile potentiality.

REMOVING THE BUSINESS CONTEXT

The above discussion may seem to constantly refer to profit-making activities, but this need not be so. In fact, such an assumed orientation may simply get in the way of creating opportunities for our students to learn. From my own perspective, it is the development of the reasonable adventurer that dictates my focus. Thus, I want my graduates to be capable of creating their opportunities for satisfaction, in any context. If we consider entrepreneurial activity to be merely a process of social change, we lower the cost of participating in the game that is entrepreneurship. It is important to appreciate that any individual or collective resource profile can exist without a profit motive. In fact it is the assumption of profit that may significantly raise the cost of entry to the process of entrepreneurship.

Consider the following example. My students were challenged to use their own collective resources to conceive an approach to raise donations for several national and local charities. They could not use any financial resources, but could call upon favours, use their existing knowledge and exploit the social contacts they had. Across the class, they had little difficulty in raising several thousand dollars for the charities. Again, those that succeeded tended to use the collective resources that were *natural* to their group. They gained enormous satisfaction and confidence from their efforts. Through creating and capturing this new value they experienced a process rich in entrepreneurial activity to reflect upon. It is at this point in time that their learning surfaced. The doing part of the activity was a sense-making process, whereas the critiquing procedure was the culmination of the learning process.

Repeating these types of challenges over and over with the students enables their learning from one challenge to be transferred to the next. Their confidence and enthusiasm for participating increase as they gain a capacity for entrepreneurial behaviour. Such challenges can be as simple as giving each group five dollars and telling them to report back with a report of the value they conceived, created and captured. Importantly they are learning about themselves and their ability to marshal resources, to work with other people and to sell, but more on that in the following chapter. For now, let us consider the implications for educators of focusing upon the students' resource profiles.

EDUCATOR IMPLICATIONS

How we as educators understand the issue of resource profiles clearly will influence our approach. If we assume that social capital is developed from connecting to pre-existing social networks, then its development is simple, connect to the right people. Alternatively, we could assume that social capital is largely latent and opportunity dependent. Likewise, access to forms of financial capital may be required for one opportunity but not another. The same applies to human capital, where the existence of expertise may also be largely opportunity dependent. Clearly, an important implication is that resource profiles are not developed from scratch, they are built from what exists and their composition changes in value from idea to idea, from collective group to collective group.

However, as Nigel Culkin, Head of Enterprise and Entrepreneurship at the University of Hertfordshire in the UK noted, it all depends on whether we are teaching about or for entrepreneurship. This critical point has been discussed earlier, but nevertheless remains of great importance. Across the responses to this issue in the IE Survey, concerns were raised as to whether the skills associated with developing a resource profile can be taught or assessed, whilst others felt this issue was beyond the scope of undergraduate students.

Let us first consider the notion of teaching about entrepreneurship in this regard. Luis Rivera Oyola, a Director of the Entrepreneurship Development Program at the University of Puerto Rico, argues that students can learn about resource profiles through the inclusion of modelling and case studies. Whereas Dr Susan Rushworth of the Swinburne University of Technology in Melbourne suggests it is very important to teach our students how to understand the value of such resources. Along the same lines, Dr Robert Morrison of the University of Texas Pan American in the United States feels that as educators we must impress the importance of networking and personal initiative to actively seek out contacts and foster strategic relationships. Or as Associate Professor Karen Sames of St. Catherine University in the United States succinctly stated, we need to help our students to see possibilities.

So how might we help our students to see possibilities? Professor Luke Pittaway of Georgia Southern University in the United States senses that it is important to show how entrepreneurs do this by bringing them into the classroom and by providing experiential opportunities for students to learn this themselves. His orientation towards experiential forms of education was noted by many other respondents. Many respondents also felt that it was important for us as educators to lead by example. Julie Logan, Professor of entrepreneurship at Cass Business School in London, felt that as educators we need to be aware of the value of such resources and demonstrate how these are assembled by bringing entrepreneurs into our classes to discuss such things. Charlotte Carey of Birmingham City University in the UK argues that educators need to develop their own resource profile and work on ways to encourage or help students to develop theirs. Going one step further, Therese Moylan at the Dun Laoghaire Institute of Art Design & Technology in Ireland, suggests that educators should lead by example and use their own social and human capital to create learning scenarios and projects for our students. Lastly, Professor Howard Frederick of Deakin University in Australia argues that educators should facilitate the creation of seed funds for student projects. A sentiment shared by Professor Lars Kolvereid at the Bodø Graduate School of Business in Norway, who would like to see educators mentor their students, help them create networks and be potentially an investor in their projects.

A closely related type of response from educators in the IE Survey was the notion that we need to specifically teach our students how to develop their social, human and financial capitals. Dr Rob Fuller, Director of Entrepreneur Development Programs, Rady School of Management, University of California, San Diego, was typical of such responses, noting the importance of helping students understand how to build social, human and financial capital, and how to creatively access resources they don't own. Other respondents noted the importance of institution links and alumni relationships in achieving this task. However, whilst there was a consensus that it is important for students to have the opportunity to *learn about how*, it was not possible to discern how such a goal might be pursued.

However, one group of respondents were very clear regarding how such learning could take place. These respondents seem to have collectively adopted an extension of Nike's *just do it* motto by arguing students should *just use it*. Dr Paula Englis at Berry College in the United States summed up much of this line of thinking, suggesting that we need to help our students realise their own potential based on *their* experiences. Peter Kraan at TSiBA Education in South Africa encourages his students to use their own networks and capital in entrepreneurship projects. Monica Kreuger, President of Global Infobrokers in Canada, suggests creating opportunities and challenges for our students to connect and network through invitations to business events; participation in volunteer activities; participation in business associations; learning how to network well (or listen effectively) and then how to develop relationships. Reflecting upon the nature of the IE Survey responses, I am again struck by the importance of one's teaching philosophy that implicitly is hidden in the responses. Whereas some educators are fully geared towards their students learning *for* and *through* (or *in*) enterprise, others seem more focused upon their students learning *about* aspects of enterprise. Let us reflect upon your situation with this last observation as a starting point.

DEVELOPING AWARENESS AND UNDERSTANDING

Clearly there is a need to let students learn *about* enterprise as well as *for* and *through* (or *in*) enterprise. The context of every module, every class and every subject area cannot be action oriented. However, and acknowledging my own biases revealed in this chapter, the development of a student's resource profile, or at least awareness of its embryonic form, would seem to require some unique form of active behaviour[3] that can be reflected upon. The first limiting factor in this regard will likely be the educator's teaching philosophy. The institutional context will also impact upon the development of suitable learning activities. Also, the collective nature of the learning outcomes related to the overall curriculum will matter as well. Let us consider each of these issues.

As discussed in Chapter 1, we teach who we are,[4] so who are you? Are you guided by gut instinct, informed by the literature, a blind experimenter, someone who is influenced by colleagues, or a combination of all of these things? How far advanced is your academic career? Are you in charge of the domain of your teaching, or supervised by others? Are you currently or have you ever been an entrepreneur? Your answers to these questions should provide clues as to how your teaching philosophy may relate to your use of experiential education techniques from which student reflection is possible. Further, are you comfortable to allow unexpected outcomes to occur in your teaching environment? Clearly the more we invite students to immerse themselves in an authentic entrepreneurial experience the less control we hold over the students' learning outcomes. Given that our students cannot all develop the same resource profile, facilitating such divergent learning outcomes makes perfect sense. Perhaps at this point in time you feel comfortable with what is being suggested? Alternatively, perhaps you feel restricted from the opportunity to develop such open processes? The key issue I feel is to ensure you have a reference point that you can call home. A set of coordinates that you remain connected to. Why might this be important? You need to be able to make sense of the changes you introduce relative to conditions that existed prior to your actions. If you are able to explain the nature of the outcomes that arise after you have acted, you are well placed to decide what is worth retaining, what needs adjusting and what should be dispensed with. It's what entrepreneurs do every day when making decisions in the absence of complete information. We too need to be capable of using our own cognitive heuristics to advance the learning opportunities for our students. We cannot know in advance exactly what is required, only the outcomes we choose to pursue on their behalf. In the absence of the confidence required to serve your students as you sense they should be served, a well-chosen mentor may make this journey into the unknown much easier. The next issue is the institutional context.

As previously discussed in Chapter 1, a range of dialogic relationships will most definitely influence your ability to teach. They cannot be ignored, and we must respect the presence of such relationships. How will you create legitimacy for your students' activities vis-à-vis the accepted institutional norms that surround you? It can be a tough challenge, but just as entrepreneurs battle to develop cognitive and socio-political legitimacy[5] for their goods and services every day in society, so must we. There is an old African saying, if you want to go quickly go alone, if you want to go far, go together. If I have learnt anything during the past few years it is that you cannot fight the legitimacy battle alone, you must arm yourself with wise friends. Again, collecting well-chosen mentors is an excellent way to enable you to progress your agenda. We are all faced with the challenge that the fantastic ideas we come across at conferences, in journals or through networking are not always that easy to transfer into our institutional contexts. The process of introducing any such change is however precisely that which we encourage our students to learn. In short, it is easier to overcome institutional barriers by being an entrepreneur than as a well-meaning educator. Whilst it is the educator who will develop the nature of the learning outcomes and accompanying learning activities, it may well be the entrepreneur within you that succeeds in winning the battle for your students.

This brings us to the last suggested limiting factor, what is it you wish for your students to achieve? The very scope of your efforts and their quest are essentially entwined in the course/subject learning outcomes you develop. Clearly, the learning outcomes related to individual subjects and/or across your course will impact your ability to offer authentic learning experiences through which awareness of and/or development of the student's resource profile is possible. If you limit your learning outcomes to *you will learn about the importance of resource profiles* rather than *you will have the opportunity to reflect upon the development of your resource profile*, the types of learning activities will differ greatly. Thus, your ability to create authentic learning experiences that connect back neatly into your strategically developed learning outcomes is very important. We must always remember that the learning outcomes belong to the students, not to the educators. With this in mind, we should aim to ensure the same is true for the learning activities; let the students *just use it*. The next issue for discussion is the process and importance of students learning to sell.

NOTES

1.   See Aldrich and Martinez (2001) for a detailed discussion of the components and value of entrepreneurs' resource profiles.
2.   See Smilor (1997).
3.   In the sense that such activities may not typically be seen as pedagogically sound in comparison to other more lecturer-driven subjects.
4.   See Palmer (1997).
5.   See Aldrich and Martinez (2001) for their discussion of the importance of all forms of legitimacy and their contribution to determining entrepreneurial success or otherwise.

PART III

Being Entrepreneurial

8.   The Art of Selling

Marketing is not selling. These were the first words that jumped off the page as I read my first ever text book as a mature age university student. Up until that point in my life, I was convinced that selling was marketing. How could I have got it so wrong? On reflection, I now feel very sure that I really didn't get it too wrong, but rather the standard approach to positioning the process of marketing in higher education was (and still is) misdirected. Sure, there are clearly differences between marketing per se and entrepreneurial marketing,[1] but what about the importance of selling? In my experience entrepreneurs that cannot sell are severely limited in the roles they can play in the process of entrepreneurship.

Again, I accept my personal biases may be distorting my approach to this issue. However, I have always held the view that selling is the most fundamental of business skills because it permeates across every level of business. From gaining peoples' confidence to being trusted starting a new venture, to communicating a vision, to understanding how to work with people, to understanding what consumer pain your efforts will heal. Serial entrepreneur Barry Moltz of Chicago says people only buy when they're in pain; I agree. I would much prefer that my students graduate with the capacity to understand how to sense and respond to *pain* in society than know the five or six steps to this or that marketing process. I want my students to be able to sense problems and offer solutions that are communicated in such a way that they are acceptable. This chapter therefore is focused on the art of selling; it unashamedly celebrates the importance of selling.

THE CONTEXT OF SELLING

Previously, I used the mantra, *we teach who we are*, and I also believe it is true *we sell (and buy) who we are*. On the basis of this logic, we need to ensure our students know themselves. I hold the view (strict hierarchies aside) that there is virtually no form of human interaction that cannot be distilled into a moment of selling. Again, it is useful to dispense with aligning selling to a purely business context. Anytime we try to convince others of our point of view we are selling. When my daughter was seven years old, she frequently used to suggest that my son (then a one year old) looked like he needed an ice cream. What she was cleverly attempting to do was to use my emotional ties to my infant son to gain an ice cream for herself as well. It was interesting to watch one child making sense of how she could gain something from facilitating something else. When all is said and done, she was trying to sell something. It is from within this context that I wish to discuss selling; the capacity to persuade others to think or act in ways that attract a benefit to the selling agent. My argument is simple: if you can master selling in all manner of day to day situations, you will have developed the prerequisite skills to sell successfully in business. So let us return to the issue of knowing one's self.

Early during my career I was introduced to many ideas and concepts related to selling. Many were fads and many related to sound underlying ways of making sense of the opportunities we are confronted with to persuade others of our way of thinking. Without doubt, the ideas that have had the most impact, and have since been enjoyed by my students, are those that relate to understanding temperament types. When I first started reading David Keirsey's[2] wonderful book, *Please Understand Me*, I was truly enlightened. I became empowered; I was able to think my way through opportunistic moments in time as if they were unfolding in slow motion, because I was able to see clues as to what types of pain were on offer to be healed. Let us first consider the nature of David Keirsey's ideas to lay a foundation for what is to follow.

THE FOUR TEMPERAMENTS

Keirsey states that a person's temperament is a configuration of observable personality traits, such as habits of communication, patterns of action, and sets of characteristic attitudes, values and talents.[3] The interplay between personality, temperament and character is illustrated in Figure 8.1. Keirsey also argues that temperament relates to personal needs, the nature of workplace behaviour and the general roles performed in society. Let's step through the relationships illustrated in Figure 8.1.

Our personality is said to have two separate but interrelated properties, temperament and character. Whereas temperament relates to a configuration of our inborn pre-dispositions, our character is a configuration of our habits of life. Habits that may be altered through interaction with the environments we encounter. So whilst our temperament is relatively hardwired into our brain, our character emerges over time ontogenetically as our temperament continually interacts with its environs. Importantly, Keirsey emphasises 'that temperament, character, and personality are configured, which means that, not only are we predisposed to develop certain attitudes and not others, certain actions and not others, but that these actions and attitudes are unified, they hang together'.[4] Further, we observe that they *hang together* to produce identifiably different forms of behaviour; forms of behaviour that seemingly tend to map into four types.

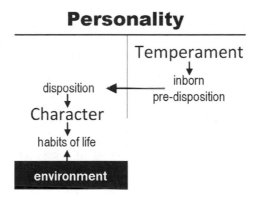

Figure 8.1   A configuration of personality, temperament and character

The challenge for our students is to understand how their temperament will impact upon the nature of their social relations. We as educators can create multiple forms of interaction through which students must navigate a task or landscape using their knowledge of who they are vis-à-vis those they encounter. This should represent an opportunity to have fun and to learn from experience. In this respect, such types of learning processes offered to your students should be repeated so that they can learn within and between such experiences. So, let us now move forward to consider what discernible elements can be identified as comprising each student's temperament.

I will strictly confine the focus of my discussion to four temperament elements: sanguine, choleric, phlegmatic and melancholy. Whilst I acknowledge these labels relate to other elements used within alternative frameworks for discussing temperaments, I choose to use these for a very simple reason. Experience demonstrates that students can identify with and use these four elements to develop a sound appreciation of how their personality impacts positively and negatively across a range of social situations. That is, situations within which they invariably have opportunities to sell. A raft of resources are available to educators to support the adoption of such (or other alternative) elements. These elements were first labelled by

Galen in 190 AD. Let us consider the primary assumptions about each element including further consideration as to the implications for graduate entrepreneurship.[5]

The Sanguine

The sanguine temperament relates to a pre-disposition towards sociable and inspiring behaviour. Indeed, sociability is the bedrock upon which other traits flow. They are outgoing, comfortable in seemingly any social situation, gifted with a carefree attitude of taking things as they come. As such, they tend to be extraverted and relatively emotionally stable. In the working environment they tend to contribute free-flowing original thoughts and seek to inspire others to do so as well. They are highly optimistic dreamers who think big, ideally suited to conceptualising a start-up opportunity. However, they have the ability to be quite reckless, with a short-term focus on temporary ideas resulting in an apparent lack of long-term conviction to follow through on even their most passionate convictions. Nevertheless, they are generally blessed with a unique capacity to engage in endless forms of imagination.

The Choleric

The choleric temperament relates to a pre-disposition towards assertive and goal-oriented behaviour. There is a competitive edge that prevails alongside endless energy to achieve. They share the sanguine optimism but can be far more aggressive in the pursuit of their dreams. They have a tendency to tackle issues head on, refusing to budge on deadlines and pre-determined objectives. They long for high pressured work environments that are action oriented, and are strong candidates for start-up activities. Their potential downside is an inability to work with other people, there is always the possibility of demonstrations of unstable emotional behaviour. As a temperament, the choleric must mature through adolescence to ensure they shed their bullying tendencies. However, when all is said and done, they can be very impressive in their ability to get things done. The only question being, at what cost?

The Phlegmatic

The phlegmatic temperament relates to a pre-disposition towards thoughtful and controlled behaviour. They are the relationship builders, supporters of other people. They operate best in environments based upon trust, mutual respect and shared meaning. They too also tend to be quite emotionally stable despite the artefacts of such behaviour sometimes remaining bashfully hidden. They have a tendency to work in environments that support the work of others and/or a non-profit focus. They regularly contribute their time to volunteering. They can be perceived as indecisive, lacking motivation or the courage to stand up for their convictions. Such judgements, commonly made within the context of a moment of opportunity to act, belie the fact that the phlegmatic likes to think and listen and then mull things over before acting. Unfortunately, sometimes others have already moved on when they have finally made their minds up. Nevertheless, their patience is a virtue, an asset that the sanguine and choleric could frequently use more often.

The Melancholy

The melancholy temperament relates to a pre-disposition towards cautious, methodical and efficient behaviour. Despite a tendency towards relatively pessimistic behaviour, the melancholy orientation brings with it the confidence and surety of a process orientation, something sadly lacking from the free and easy approach of the sanguine. However, their inflexibility and pursuit of perfection can get in the way of making valued contributions in team environments. They are well suited to occupations like engineering, medicine and legal work where attention to detail is of utmost importance. However, a tendency towards being too rigid and overly process oriented sometimes gets in the way of their skills being applied to useful effect.

However, the above reference to the four temperaments does not in any way suggest that any one person is only pre-disposed towards the traits of that particular orientation, as discussed above. As evidenced from the brief description of the four temperaments, each has its own distinctive qualities and shortcomings. However, they are operationalised in a blended process whereby most people have varying combinations of the four temperaments that recombine and alter across different situations and the course of life in general. At any moment in time a particular combination of temperaments is evidenced by *what we say and what we do*. Thus, we transmit clues that explain our current and future intentions; clues that our students can be taught to find and understand.

DEVELOPING THE INSTINCT OF THE SALESPERSON

The process of selling something could simply be described as moments of recognition (or signals) that feed instantaneously into how we offer something to others for consideration. Our challenge as educators is 1) to ensure that our students have a heightened sense of the clues that surround them, and 2) that they are capable of responding in the blink of an eye to *what* is being offered to *whom* for consideration. To the extent that we can assist our students to develop these high-end skills we will have succeeded in addressing the importance of selling. Let me share with you the nature of the processes used to develop such advanced skills at UTAS.

Since 2002, a subject related to the process of creativity has operated at UTAS. Arising naturally from this subject has been an increasing focus on the process of selling. I say naturally as the process of creative problem solving requires of its participants the ability to sell generated solutions to identified or assumed stakeholders. Thus, a specific focus upon knowing one's own temperament and how it plays out in different types of situations is a fundamental starting point for every student's development. The process begins with a simple temperament test[6] from which each student's temperament is self-evaluated. Once the student is armed with information relating to their temperament, they are given multiple opportunities to interact with other class members and then reflect upon the nature of such interaction vis-à-vis their temperament. Typically, one of the first learning activities the students are involved in is creative problem-solving presentations.

CREATIVE PROBLEM SOLVING

Solving problems using creativity is a mixture of seriousness and fun. It is an appreciation of the interaction between these two dispositions that creates the perfect playground for students to learn about temperaments. The process is suggested to relate to four discrete, yet interrelated steps. First (working in small groups), students need to redefine an actual problem. There is little point trying to generate novel and unique ideas for problems that don't matter. During this phase, it is the logical judgement of the student that must come to the fore. Second, with a clear understanding of the problem/challenge that requires attention, the students are clear to use their creativity to generate a raft of possible ideas. During this phase, logical judgement has been banished, replaced with the freedom to suggest without fear of judgement. Third, armed with a raft of potential solutions the students must invite judgement back into the process. The merits of each idea generated must be considered in the context of the actual problem/challenge being focused upon. Fourth, having chosen an idea to address the problem/challenge, the task remains to *sell* the solution. It is at this point in time when the nature of what is being sold to whom becomes of critical importance. It is through the process of pitching the idea that the students are able to internalise their understanding of the temperaments. Repeated over and over, this process awakens within the students an innate capacity to sell. The challenge throughout this simple process is to help the students to engage and disengage their use of judgement so as to gain focus and to also be freed from the restrictions of such judgement.

Accompanying this task simultaneously is the process of group sense making outlined previously in Chapter 5. This process provides students with access to the means to deeply reflect upon their feelings and understanding of their temperament. A process that operates in parallel to the various learning activities used to develop their selling skills. The availability of such a reflective process is argued to be pivotal in creating deeper awareness and acceptance of one's temperament and also creating the source of consideration from which to attempt to alter one's habits of life. The next task used to stimulate the development of selling skills is a mystery concept challenge.

Mystery Concept Challenge

Students working in small groups are confronted with an abstract image that could conceivably be several things. The image is chosen on the basis that it does not represent anything in particular. The students are then challenged by four questions. What is it? Who is the target market? How is it positioned? How much start-up capital? These four questions are to be answered via a short presentation to their fellow students. The context for the task is always set against one of the four temperaments. So the students must conceive something of value which could be communicated to a particular type of personality. They need to present in a style that is in sync with the requirements of that particular temperament. Importantly, they are exposed to the efforts of their fellow students, and so their learning experience is not limited solely by the interpretation of the situation. Where others excel beyond their abilities, they gain from understanding the efforts of others to sell a concept. Alternatively, if we remove the mystery from the challenge, we have an opportunity to see their selling skills laid bare for all to see.

The Trading Game

Several years ago my classes were increasingly being divided into domestic students and overseas students. The integration of these two groups didn't seem to occur naturally. My solution to this issue was to devise a game that would require high levels of socialisation and selling to be successful. The subsequent trading game has now become a traditional challenge for my students to conquer. The game[7] is very simple, yet by the nature of its development, requires from each student a commitment to understanding the needs and the situation of their fellow students in order to succeed. Let us consider the rules of the game.

	Card 1	Card 2	Card 3	Card 4	Card 5	Card 6
Item A	10	3	7	0	1	5
Item B	7	10	1	3	5	0
Item C	3	7	10	5	0	1
Item D	1	0	5	10	7	3
Item E	0	5	3	1	10	7
Item F	5	1	0	7	3	10

Figure 8.2   The trading game

Illustrated above in Figure 8.2 are six columns of numbers, all totalling 26 in value arranged in different combinations across six items. Each column represents one of six different cards that students may receive when playing the game. For instance, card 1 has items A to F in the following order; 10, 7, 3, 1, 0 and 5. The aim of the game is to attempt to trade your card's numbers (horizontally) up to a higher value. For example, if I am playing card 1, I would want to find a student with card 5 so that I could trade my Item E for their Item E, thus gaining the difference between my 0 and their 10, for a net gain of 10. As the game progresses, and the highly sort after 10s are traded away, I might also like to trade my Item C with a student holding card 2, so that I could increase the value of my Item C from 3 to 7, therefore making a net gain of 4. The challenge of course is that you will have to give up something in order to gain what you require. However, the difference between what you have to trade and what you eventually receive is your salesmanship.

Played repeatedly, the trading game requires of the students the development and execution of strategy, plus the development and maintenance of healthy, profitable relationships with *all* students in the class. Throughout this process, the students are alone in their efforts to conquer the game, but amongst friends in terms of the development of their strategies. But ultimately, it is the student as an individual who is learning by doing.

Alternatively, another way in which students learn from each other is in the deconstructing of their efforts to conceive value.

DECONSTRUCTING CONCEIVED VALUE

An important element of selling is preparation; understanding the task at hand, or put simply, having an accurate insight into the needs of your target market. This is a problematic process when left in the theoretical domain. It is important that our students get out to meet their assumed customers. That our students are confronted with the true reality of their customers' needs. A process I have used previously (within the context of the 4Cs approach) is to require the students to plan and deliver an event. Recently, my students were required to run a restaurant for one sitting, in a theme/format of their choosing. Every fortnight the students would attend class and discuss their progress in the planning of their event. My role as educator was to assist them through supportive suggestions and also to question the wisdom of their espoused logic.

Throughout our conversations it became clear that meeting face-to-face with representatives of the assumed target market was the last task they expected to do. There was a Field of Dreams like mantra in operation; *if we organise it, they will come.* The potential value in developing pitching skills and an adaptive capacity towards different temperaments was being wasted through the refusal to include the customer into the heart of their planning. This was not an issue of laziness; the students clearly demonstrated their capacity to apply themselves to organising their planned events. However, the one fundamental task the students tended to avoid was getting up and close with their assumed target market. I sensed that at times they didn't want to risk meeting their future customers and risking the chance of someone raining on their parade. Sound familiar? It is not uncommon for entrepreneurs to be so blinded by their passion for their new venture that they will not risk criticism of their plans. However, for our students, we must ensure their date with destiny is not postponed. We have a responsibility to ensure their ambitions and capabilities collide with the reality of the world they wish to create.

There is a simple process that can aid this process. By requiring of our students to question their fellow students' plans vis-à-vis the assumptions in play regarding their potential customers, they can deconstruct each others' plans. They can also assist each other to reconstruct their plans as well. Throughout this process, we are again the guide on the side, ready to offer mentoring support without overly imposing our views. They key is to let them find their own flaws and to find a pathway forward from which to

correct any such flaws. In this way their instinct as to actual customer value
is being honed through their deliberation rather than from merely accepting
advice from their ever-wise educator. One last process that my students
engage in is the trading up of items.

Trading Items Up

What if we could strip our students bare and leave them with nothing else but
their sales instincts to survive upon? What if we were to make this a serious
part of the students' assessment? At UTAS this is exactly what we have done
in our creativity unit. Working in small groups, each group has been given a
chocolate bar that must be traded into something of increased value. Once
this first initial trade has taken place, the new item must then also be traded
for something of increased value, and so on. Each group is required to keep a
trade register to record their trades. This process occurs across the entire
semester and during each fortnightly workshop each group must present their
trade register to the other groups. Professor Luke Pittaway of
Georgia Southern University in Savannah has previously used a similar
activity at the University of Sheffield in the UK. He felt that a trading
competition is a great way to test students' entrepreneurial skills in a fun and
interactive way, further noting that the competition helps students with both
their selling and negotiation skills, as well as giving them the opportunity to
learn entrepreneurship in an exciting way.

At UTAS, each group is assessed in three ways. First, they are assessed on
the basis of the volume of trades they have completed relative to the other
groups in the class. Second, they are assessed on the basis of the percentage
increase in the value of the item held at the end of the fortnight relative to the
other groups in the class. Third, they are assessed on the basis of the actual
value of the item held at the end of the fortnight relative to the other groups
in the class. In total, 50% of the marks for the subject relate to their
performance in this task. It is the primary focus of their efforts. Selling (via
trading items) is the absolute challenge the students face to excel in the
subject. The subject offers them an opportunity to put into practice the selling
techniques related to sensing the temperament clues related to each trading
situation.

In summary, we cannot directly teach our students how to sell, but we can
create the environment within which they can learn about themselves and
develop selling skills. I say this not to lessen the role of the educator, but
rather to highlight the problem of the educator getting in the way of their
students' opportunities to develop such valuable skills. It's not to say that the
activities described above are truly unique, they are not. However, I believe
that deliberately arming the students with a skill set that can be used

repeatedly across these learning activities is. As we have done in previous chapters, let us now consider how the issue of selling plays out globally.

THE ACCEPTANCE AND DEMAND OF SELLING SKILLS

The overwhelming majority of respondents to the IE Survey agreed that the development of selling skills should be a fundamental component of EE. However, the assertion that such skills are actually developed in higher education is still open for debate. There were some opinions expressed that entrepreneurs don't sell, that they merely develop systems that convey solutions to identified parties who have a need. Alternatively, others were concerned that academics may be weak in the area of sales skills and/or expertise. Overall, it would seem that the importance of developing sales skills is widely supported, but confidence as to how to do so is not so clear.

Again the issue of dialogic relationships comes to the fore. Professor Luke Pittaway of Georgia Southern University in the United States noted they have a Sales Center with a large number of courses on sales – courses that are increasingly being built into the entrepreneurship programme with students encouraged to take such courses as electives. Clearly in this situation the value of existing structures can be tapped into. However, sometimes we as educators are trapped within the structures of pre-existing approaches and cultures. Professor Pi-Shen Seet of Flinders University in Australia argues that someone needs to teach people how to sell. He felt that too often marketing courses focus too much on marketing management and market research, with entrepreneurship courses focusing on business planning, with little or nothing about selling. Again, the assumption that selling is beneath the gamut of the business school.

One issue that was mentioned by many of the IE Survey respondents was the associated development of confidence by students mastering selling skills. Logically, this makes sense. If our students become more aware of their ability to interact with others in a persuasive manner, such confidence can be used in the future endeavours. This relates back neatly to the ontological issues discussed in Chapter 3. Given that our students' entrepreneurial adventures may lie well beyond their graduation from higher education it's important that we can skill them up to *make their own way*. Clearly, having the confidence and capacity to sell themselves across a range of circumstances is central to their advancement in life. Let us now step back and consider the opportunities and challenges that you may stumble upon in this respect.

Plotting the Way Forward

I challenge you to return to my fundamental critique of your (explicit or implicit) teaching philosophy, *we teach who we are*. When it comes to selling, who are you? How does your past experience in selling factor into your current approach to teaching entrepreneurship? What type of source inputs contribute to your teaching? Are you locked into teaching someone else's curriculum, or are you the master of your own destiny? Do you hold opposing views as to the importance of students developing selling skills? These are just a few questions from where we can start the process of contemplating the way forward on this issue.

SO WHO ARE YOU?

Can you accept that *who you are* will in all likelihood significantly influence the dialogic relations between you and your students? To what extent do you demonstrate (or encourage) a culture of intellectual curiosity? Drawing on Dewey's[8] past musing on this issue, we can see how we as educators can create the conditions under which our students' curiosity to solve selling-related problems can evolve into a form of intellectual freedom. That is, I suggest the key to which the subject of and capacity for selling are held to be an intellectual challenge by our students. So where does this issue sit in your ranking of enterprising skills that should be developed? Are selling skills an educational outcome or enabling skills that influence educational outcomes? Again, I argue, who you are matters. Whilst our students can play a role in co-creating the learning environments they operate within, we as the educator remain the most dominant figure in this space. Our influence exceeds theirs as it should, but our resistance to certain issues may also restrict their learning in ways that it shouldn't. Sadly, it is not always about you when it comes to what can and can't be done.

WHERE DO YOU TEACH?

The next issue relates to the context of your teaching. Are you free to decide what is or isn't included in the curriculum your students learn within? Are you faced with the challenge of covering a range of non-negotiable topics that leaves you with little room to accommodate other softer issues, like selling? My observations in this respect are that whilst this can be a serious dilemma for many enterprise educators, it is also a relatively simple obstacle to manoeuvre around. Let's return to Biggs's idea of constructive alignment.[9] As an educator you are required to assist your students to attain the learning outcomes (determined by you or others) that are appropriate to their development. So in this first phase you may or may not have the capacity to develop a focus on selling. Let's assume for the sake of this discussion that you face limitations in this respect. Such a restriction does not spell the end of incorporating a focus on selling. The second phase of the process is related to developing learning activities through which the learning activities can be attained. Here therefore is your opportunity to incorporate forms of required behaviour from which selling skills can be developed.

Again, the nature of the dialogic relations you encounter will impact directly upon your approach to EE. However, you as an *enterprising educator* have the ability to sidestep some of the restrictions you face in order to advance the lot of your students. It is simply a case of deciding *how* your students will learn rather than *what* they will learn. So whilst all roads lead to Rome, some are more profitable to follow.

HOW INFLUENCED ARE YOU?

The results of the IE Survey clearly demonstrated an incredibly diverse and fragmented set of sources through which our EE teaching is influenced. We should celebrate this diversity, rather than defend individual sources of influence as being more appropriate than others The challenge here would seem to be ensuring you gain exposure to the teaching methods of other educators reflexively. Attending conferences is an excellent way to meet other educators in a manner that you can glean the context of their situation. Alternatively, simply contacting other educators by email/phone and requesting an opportunity to discuss their teaching with them are highly underrated approaches.

In summary, throughout this chapter I have attempted to make the case for elevating the importance of ensuring our students develop selling skills. My approach is very much about awakening awareness in each student as to their natural dispositions during personal interactions with others. By requiring of my students to sell themselves in order to succeed across a range of assessable tasks, their intellectual curiosity is heightened in ways that naturally lead to the development and retention of selling skills. An outline of the tasks used to facilitate this process has been given not to suggest they are exemplars of such activity, but rather to demonstrate the capacity of an educator to imaginatively develop and/or copy such activities. Ultimately, it will be you who must decide upon the importance of your students developing selling skills, and it will be you who must determine the most appropriate way for this to occur in the context of your teaching. The next issue for our consideration is that of idea evaluation.

NOTES

1. For an excellent overview of the differences between marketing and entrepreneurial marketing, see Bjerke and Hultman (2002).
2. See Keirsey and Bates (1984).
3. See http://www.keirsey.com.
4. Ibid.
5. To further understand the implications for graduate entrepreneurship in this regard, tap into the ideas of DeGraff and Lawrence (2002).
6. Typically I use the test on http://www.oneishy.com – it is simple to use and provides an excellent breakdown between the strengths and weaknesses of each temperament type.
7. The *Trading Game* © 2005 and support resources is freely available for use by other educators upon request.
8. See Dewey (1910: 32) for a wonderful discussion of how our students think.
9. See Biggs (2003).

9. Evaluating Ideas

It is an inescapable fact that entrepreneurs will at some point in time be surrounded by several competing ideas that vie for their attention and scarce resources. This is the reality of being entrepreneurial; an immersion in opportunities to create value. An obvious question that must be addressed therefore concerns how do EE students in higher education learn to evaluate ideas? This chapter is focused on this issue and is premised upon an approach to the issue that is informed by the ontological position outlined in Chapter 3. As such, arguments related to the order in which judgements are made so that eventual resource-dependent decisions are made are presented for your consideration. Further, an argument is being created for developing within our students a capacity for future judgment, rather than a confidence of being able to know the unknown. Importantly, this chapter represents a deliberate separation of the process of deciding upon which idea to pursue and then developing a business or action plan to pursue any chosen idea. So it is important to note that this discussion also avoids any possible conflation of personal judgement and the process of due diligence. The issue of developing a business or action plan will be addressed in the following chapter.

This discussion will be organised as follows. First we will consider the opportunities granted to EE students in higher education to evaluate entrepreneurial ideas, taking account of the global issues raised in the IE Survey. Next we will consider the ontological issues that surround such evaluative processes. Then we will discuss an alternative process that addresses the ontological issues that have been raised. Finally we will consider the opportunities that you as an EE educator have before you related to this specific issue.

IDEA EVALUATION IN HIGHER EDUCATION

The IE Survey provided overwhelming support for EE students developing the ability to evaluate ideas. Very few respondents questioned the importance of our students being able to effectively evaluate the commercial potential of new ideas. However, very few were able to articulate what are the specific implications for EE educators in this regard. Typical of the opinions expressed, Philip Clarke at Nottingham Trent University in the UK felt our challenge is to develop such evaluative skills without negatively impacting upon the innate *gut instinct* which is uniquely part of the true entrepreneurial mindset. This is an issue we need to consider in more detail. Gut instinct, what is that? Can it be taught, or is it an innate ability? Clearly a challenge here is that gut instinct typically is considered to relate to patterns of behaviour informed by past experience. Can you see the potential problem here? What if our students have no past experience evaluating ideas?

I find it interesting to note that none of the IE Survey respondents reported any pessimism regarding the ability of students to develop such evaluative skills. There would seem to be a widely held acceptance that we can teach EE students the evaluative skills required to determine the potential value of their ideas. I am still haunted by Edward De Bono's[1] assertion that there are no bad ideas, only bad judgement used to select ideas. This notion fuels my desire to avoid any conflation between personal judgement and the process of due diligence. In this vein, Dr Susan Rushworth of Swinburne University in Australia argues we should teach our students the key questions they need to address. Recognise they'll never have perfect answers, but they need to have thought about each key element so they don't make unnecessary mistakes. This sentiment sits well with me; I like the idea that we can accept the fallibility of the exercise, rather than defaulting to assumptions of objectivity, and therefore the potential development of false confidence. Let us consider the types of evaluation approaches available to EE students in higher education.

Assessing Ideas

Evaluative models exist in various forms, ranging from specialist to generalist processes. As always, context matters, evaluative frameworks that have emerged designed to assess high technology ideas should not be automatically assumed to be suitable to the evaluation of simple online business ideas. Conversely, highly generalisable frameworks may not provide an adequate means of evaluation for complex ideas.

An example of the complex nature of the evaluating of ideas can be observed in Kim and Mauborgne's Buyer Utility Map.[2] This model promotes the idea that ideas can be simultaneously developed and assessed through giving attention to the six stages of the buyer experience cycle (purchase, delivery, use, supplements, maintenance and disposal) and to six utility levers (environmental friendliness, fun/image, risk, convenience, simplicity and customer productivity). In essence, this model places an emphasis on strategic judgement to identify and build winning innovative ideas. However, the extent to which such a model is appropriate for EE students is not clear. Its stated operation occurs against a backdrop of retrospective analysis of how major players like Dell Computers and Motorola have developed past ideas. The issue of concern here relates to the capacity of EE students to genuinely understand the marketplace to which their idea would seek to breathe. Any assumption that we can recognise a winning idea in advance without having sufficient experience and/or knowledge of the idea's eventual home is, I believe, rather doubtful. The key issue here then should be what will our students learn from employing this particular evaluative process?

An alternative means of evaluation is to consider a much broader set of criteria. The late Jeff Timmons[3] provides a comprehensive screening process to assess the potential of a given idea. In all, 14 steps are required to complete the process, and to do the process justice, a significant amount of time is required to complete the process. More time than would be required to complete a standard business plan. Would such a process enable EE students to learn how to evaluate ideas, or just how to search for valuable information? This I believe is the key question.

Why are EE students evaluating ideas? Is it so that they can start a business? Is it so they can make the case for why such an idea is feasible? Is it so they can learn to choose from a variety of ideas? Is it because it is a required chapter of the text that is prescribed for their subject? Until we carefully consider such questions is it is difficult to decide upon an evaluative approach.

It has been argued that EE students could complete a two-stage process comprising first a feasibility study followed by a viability study:[4] the feasibility study providing insight into the potential to convert an idea into a business enterprise, and the viability study related to determining the potential profitability of converting the idea into a business venture. Personally, I find such processes as being too distant from the reality each EE student should traverse to evaluate their idea. This is because EE students are asked to produce knowledge typically with little more than limited personal judgement to rely upon. Under such circumstances we risk alienating our students by asking them to address too many requirements that stymie their enthusiasm for enterprise. Let's face it, in the time it takes to consider the screening process noted above, many of our students could have designed and published an online business. The world is changing, our students' needs are ever changing, and cumbersome, lengthy knowledge-seeking processes will not benefit all students. Again, the importance of choice is critical. Yes, there undoubtedly will be some students who would take great comfort from such a drawn out and methodical process. But just as only a small percentage of our students are graduating with an ongoing enterprise developed from within their EE studies, we shouldn't overplay the importance of making such evaluative processes exhaustive.

Ask yourself this question. Would you rather your EE students evaluated many ideas during their studies and became proficient at evaluation, or would you rather they evaluated one big idea? Herein lies a common problem in EE; the conflation of evaluation with business planning. I argue that we should enable both processes to exist separately; otherwise, students may get locked into a dog of an idea and be forced to persist in working on it in order to achieve a satisfactory grade. These independent, yet clearly interrelated processes do not always mix well. To better explain the paradox that exists between evaluation and planning, let us briefly return to the issue of ontology.

THE ONTOLOGICAL ISSUE

The structure of many EE texts is seemingly premised upon working towards the development of a business plan. I feel that within this form of approach a deadly assumption lurks. An assumption that students can competently evaluate the ideas they entertain. The logic behind this reasoning is simple. In the absence of competent evaluation our EE students frequently tackle the task of constructing a business plan without a sound understanding of the merits of the idea under consideration. With reference to Figure 9.1, let's unpack this assertion.

In Figure 9.1, several interrelated issues are suggested. Starting with an acceptance that EE students can learn *about*, *for*, *in* and *through* enterprise (and combinations of all four), we can envisage several contexts to their learning. I argue that when students learn primarily *about* enterprise they do so in an implied context. Likewise, when our students develop skills via learning *for* enterprise the context tends to commence within an artificial context. That is, we may allow our students to engage in forms of experiential education in a relatively safe learning environment. When EE students learn *in* enterprise (such as industry-based placements) they interact with an external context where other factors enter the realm of their EE learning. Lastly, when EE students learn *through* enterprise, it is the context of their life that impacts their learning.

In the top right hand corner of Figure 9.1, the letter 'K' stands for knowledge. It is argued that a temporal separation of the use of knowledge exists across these learning spectrums. When students learn *about* and *for*, there may be a greater focus on the future use of the knowledge they are developing, whereas the opposite is true for learning *in* and *through* enterprise.

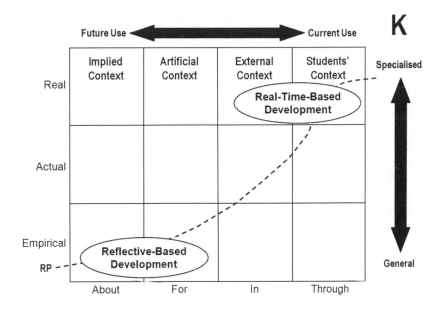

Figure 9.1 The context of enterprise knowledge

From my own personal observations the nature of the knowledge used by EE students also changes (from general to specialised) as they move within this spectrum, especially as they develop their resource profile potential. Let's pause for a moment to reintroduce the notion of a stratified reality.[5] Enlisting Roy Bhaskar's stratified reality enables us to understand the separation of the time and place in which our students' habits of thought may be altered from any future expression of enterprising behaviour at a latter point in time.

You might be asking yourself, why is the idea of a stratified reality important to evaluating ideas? I contend that typically there is spatial and temporal separation between the student's idea and the reality of its expected marketplace due to their personal circumstances. Typically, students learning *about* enterprise typically do so from afar, whereas students learning *through* enterprise may operate within the context of their idea. Thus, there may be a potential gap between what can be known and what needs to be known when students evaluate ideas. As students progress through their EE studies, it is possible that they may be located in the domain of the real, but as previously discussed, unless they are actually involved in the start-up process, this is quite unlikely. Likewise, consideration must be given to the context under which a student's resource profile may be developed. Is there a reliance upon reflective-based development or are students able to develop a resource profile in real time? Essentially, we should accept that an ontological problem exists, a problem that may prevent students from gaining access to the reality they are assumed to be able to comprehend. At UTAS, we have been steadily developing a range of choices to enable our EE students to develop quality evaluative skills that are adaptable in their application to a range of temporal settings. Let's take some time to outline the primary methodology. A reminder, this discussion of idea evaluation precedes the discussion of business plans in the following chapter. The focus of the next section is solely upon developing entrepreneurial judgement within our students, rather than any capacity for gathering and analysing data for business planning.

THE IDEAS PROCESS

Our students at UTAS are increasingly becoming adept at evaluating ideas using the IDEAS process. IDEAS, an acronym for *innovation development early assessment system*, is a structured methodology developed by my colleague, Associate Professor Jack English.[6] The aim of the process is to identify new business ideas and to develop sound judgement with regard to which ideas are worth investing more time and effort into. Developing an ability to use the IDEAS process builds upon many of the enterprising skills the students have previously acquired. For example, their understanding of the resource profile they may hold vis-à-vis any particular idea is highlighted as they use the process. To train the students to use the process, they are first introduced to a range of complementary background issues. For example, the nature of successful business ideas, the relationship of such ideas to temporal and spatial change in the general environment, and the range of business opportunities that are available to the budding entrepreneur.

There are 40 specific areas targeted for evaluation by personal judgement, as illustrated in Table 9.1. The key issue here is that we are using personal judgement throughout the entire evaluation process, so in effect the students are screening ideas for their perceived potential. Let us consider the issues which we require their personal judgement to be concentrated upon, starting with the potential demand for the idea.

Table 9.1   Focus of the IDEAS process

Potential Demand	Market Approval	Competitive Strength	Boundary Risks
Market size	Needs and wants	Differentiation	Regulatory risk
Market growth	Recognition	Value	Technology risk
Market stability	Compatibility	Customer power	Environmental risk
Sustainability	Complexity	Supplier power	Socio-economic risk
Extensions	Distribution	Competitors	Dependence risk
Establishment Risks	**Skills & Experience**	**Resources**	**Dollars & Sense**
Planning risk	Marketing expertise	Financial resources	Sales forecast
Marketing risk	Technical expertise	Physical resources	Profitability
Deliverables risk	Financial expertise	Human resources	Cost structure
Liquidity risk	Operational expertise	Intellectual resources	Financial structure
Personal risk	Managerial expertise	Network resources	Cash flow

Potential Demand

The first issue is that of *market size*, or how many potential customers are assumed to exist in the anticipated target market area? Here the students need to consider the expected patterns of consumption, average weekly spend and the nature of demographic, lifestyle, social, technological, political and economic trends. Once considered, a judgement (across five items ranging from very large to very small) is made. For each of the other 39 issues, a similar judgement is made using five issue-specific items that capture the attractiveness or unattractiveness of each issue vis-à-vis commercial potential.

The next issue is that of *market growth*, or the potential for increased demand for the service/product related to the idea. There is a need here to consider the nature of competitor relations and estimates of growth may need to be linked to considering the performance of comparable products and services. Next is the issue of *market stability*, or the relative stability of demand in the foreseeable future. Here issues of legitimacy, seasonality and the likelihood of external events need to be considered. Next, the issue of *sustainability*, or the expected commercial life, needs addressing. Are there particular short-run social trend issues related to the idea? Which point of the product life cycle is your idea related to? The last issue related to potential demand is that of *extensions*, or any additional business opportunities that can be derived from the original idea. The underlying logic is that ideas that have the potential for product/service extension have less potential risk than those that do not. Let us now consider the five issues related to market approval.

Market Approval

In terms of market approval, student judgement is required as to what basic *needs and wants* exist for their idea. How does their idea relate to intrinsic needs of the identified target market? Needs they may relate to their safety, their status, pleasure, lifestyle or convenience. So there is a requirement for students to use their judgement to account for different levels of desire that exist in our communities. The next issue is that of *recognition*, or the extent to which the features and benefits of the idea can be readily understood by the target market. So the student's judgement now relates to their understanding of the positioning possibilities and related communication issues vis-à-vis their idea. Next is the issue of *compatibility*, or the potential acceptance of the idea vis-à-vis existing attitudes and/or methods of using other products and services that relate to their idea. Next is the issue of *complexity*, or the ease with which the product or service would be used. So here students must exercise judgement as to the nature of the decision being made by the end-users. How important is the decision and what degree of unknown information relates to the idea in the end-users' minds? The last market approval issue is that of *distribution*, or the proximity of the end-user to envisaged distribution channels for the product/service. So the extent to which students understand the essence of the relationship between the idea, modes of distribution and related stakeholder behaviour will shape their judgement in this regard. Let us now consider the five issues related to competitive strength.

Competitive Strength

The first consideration of the competitive strength of the idea relates to its potential *differentiation* from other existing products or services. So consideration of the idea's features, performance, durability, functionality, style and simplicity (to name but a few points of difference) must be taken into account when forming a judgement on differentiation. The next issue relates to *value*, or the perceptions of the end-user of likely benefits from the idea. So students must make judgements about the sources of value derivable from the idea relative to existing alternatives regarding issues of differentiation, price, service, convenience and technological platforms. The next issue is that of *customer power*, or the potential for customers to negotiate for lower prices or features. So students must consider the role of customer concentration, switching costs, direct competition, high fixed costs and the nature of information about the idea available to customers. Next is the issue of *supplier power*, or the potential for suppliers to dictate the conditions surrounding the availability of inputs needed to commercialise the idea. So students must consider the role of supplier concentration, switching costs, volume, direct competition and the nature of information about the inputs required. Last, the issue of *competitors*, or those organisations that directly or indirectly offer the same or similar products or services. Therefore, students must consider the nature of the product/service, factors such as branding, existing customer relationships and access to distribution channels. Let us now consider the ten issues related to boundary and establishment risks.

Boundary Risks

The IDEAS process requires students to account for two broad types of risk, boundary and establishment risk. The first of the five identified boundary risks is *regulatory risk*, or the extent to which the idea is legal, safe and meets other regulatory requirements. Next is the issue of *technology risk*, or the extent to which the idea may be susceptible to changes in technology. The next issue is that of *environmental risk*, or the extent to which the idea's development would produce an impact on the environment. Next, the issue of *socio-economic risk*, or the extent the idea might be hampered by social or economic force. The last boundary risk issue is that of *dependence risk*, or the extent to which the idea's development is linked to the presence of other products, processes or services. Thus, boundary risks relate to factors that are typically beyond the control of the student, which nevertheless can restrict the commercial potential of their idea. Let us now consider the five establishment risks.

Establishment Risks

The process of converting any idea into a genuine business opportunity will always include a range of inherent risks related to the decisions our students make. The first establishment risk is *planning risk*, or the degree to which the idea's development is actually supported by a plan involving concrete tactics. The next issue is *marketing risk*, or the extent to which the student truly understands the needs and wants of the assumed target market and the nature of the marketplace they wish to enter. Next, is *deliverables risk*, or the ability of the student to produce something that delivers the value as promised, and if they are able to develop the business structures required to exploit the idea. The next issue is *liquidity risk*, or the extent to which the necessary finances can be acquired to exploit the idea at start-up and through initial development. The last issue is *personal risk*, or the extent to which the student would be prepared to expose their finances, time and personal relations to considerable strain. The last remaining fifteen issues relate to the business model required to develop the idea.

Skills and Experience

The next area of focus is upon the required skills and/or experience necessary to move the idea into the marketplace. The first issue students must form a judgement upon is that of *marketing expertise*, or the capacity to make the right decisions to develop and deliver the right benefits to the right end-users. Then, students must consider the issue of *technical expertise*, or the required skills and knowledge necessary to design, develop and deliver the product or service. The next issue is *financial expertise*, or knowledge of how to manage the financial resources required to commercialise the idea. This is followed by the issue of *operational expertise*, or the capacity to manage a range of straightforward and complex tasks related to commercialise the idea. Lastly, the issue of *managerial expertise*, or a requirement to work on the business rather than merely in the business. Let us now consider the five resource issues.

Resources

As noted previously, the resource profile of the student entrepreneur is of paramount importance. The IDEAS process provides a direct focus on five types of resources. The first issue is *financial resources*, or the extent to which the idea under question needs to be supported by capital. Next, the issue of *physical resources*, or the extent to which physical resources are required to support the commercialisation of the idea. This is followed by the issue of *human resources*, or the degree to which there are staffing issues and/or access to particular skilled types of labour. The next issue is *intellectual resources*, or the extent to which the idea's development relates to specialised knowledge and/or intellectual property. The last resource issue is that of *network resources*, or the degree to which the idea's development is reliant upon external assistance. Let us now consider the last five issues of the IDEAS process.

Dollars and Sense

The last set of issues relates to the degree a business model can be accurately developed to explain the financial potential of the idea. The first issue is that of a *sales forecast*, or the confidence that a true measure of future sales could (or should) be formulated. The next issue is that of *profitability*, or the degree of confidence of an expected profit from commercialising the idea. The next issue relates to *cost structure*, or the extent to which confidence can be expressed in achieving a sound contribution margin and low fixed costs. The next issue is *financial structure*, or the ability to rely upon current assets to finance the idea's development rather than seeking other forms of financing, such as equity or debt financing. The last issue is that of *cash flow*, or the extent of time between commercialisation and positive cash flows.

Figure 9.2   Output of the IDEAS process

So, students are required to make 40 judgements that collectively produce a graphical profile of the commercial potential of the idea, as depicted in Figure 9.2 above. This profile also relates to a commercial feasibility rating ranging out of 100. Ideas rated below 60 are assumed too low for further consideration, ideas rated 60 to 79 are considered marginal, and ideas rated 80 to 100 are considered worthy of more time and effort to further research their potential. The key issue here is that every EE student has the capacity to form judgements across each of the 40 questions. The judgements may be formed on gut instinct, from personal experience or from common sense. The key here is not to see the outcome of the process as a final determination that an idea is great, good or bad, but rather that individual or competing ideas can be evaluated for potential using a robust process.

In summary, our experience shows that as students become practised with the IDEAS process they can evaluate ideas in less than an hour. This is of great value because we can encourage our students to canvas multiple ideas during their studies, rather than requiring them to adopt an idea prematurely to act as a host for the purpose of completing a feasibility/business plan. The last section of this chapter is focused upon the opportunities that EE educators have before them on this specific issue.

REFLECTING UPON YOUR STUDENTS' ABILITIES

Once again the nature of your teaching philosophy is important to your approach to idea evaluation. Several issues are worthy of your reflection. For instance, how many subjects are your students engaged in prior to evaluating an idea? Could it be the case that they will be completing an enterprise subject as an elective choice and perhaps learning more *about* enterprise than *for*, *in* or *through* enterprise? If so, and assuming they are required to evaluate the potential of an entrepreneurial idea, how will you overcome their likely inability to acquire the information to evaluate the idea?

If your aim is to develop an understanding of the process of evaluating an idea, how many times does the process need to be attempted before any such understanding can be properly developed? The IDEAS process discussed here illustrates a simple and effective way of allowing students to evaluate multiple ideas simultaneously or separately. It requires of the student no more than the latent judgement they walk around with every day. If you consider the means of evaluation available to your students, to what extent are you assuming the evaluative process is hosted within a business planning process, such as constructing a feasibility/business plan?

Contemplating these issues requires us to step back and consider the nature of the learning outcomes we deem appropriate for our students. If the learning outcomes relate to learning how to evaluate ideas, why allow the process of constructing a business plan to get in the way? Alternatively, if we truly desire for our students the ability to develop a well-researched business plan, on what basis have we determined the appropriateness of the idea to which such planning belongs? Again, I contend there is an ontological issue here that cannot be ignored. Certain types of learning situations do not lend themselves to the attainment of knowledge essential to the development of a sound business plan. Add to this dilemma the problem of the diversity of the student cohorts we confront vis-à-vis their experience, aspirations, local knowledge and capacities to learn and we have a potential problem. The solution that has been offered for consideration here is to use a universal process that separates idea evaluation from business plan development. Again, such matters are issues upon which you need to decide what is best for your students' learning within the context of your subject, the course it belongs to, the nature of the students you encounter and the nature of your teaching philosophy.

In summary, there is no escaping the influence of your teaching philosophy with respect to your approach to this matter. Hopefully you can see the logic in the approach outlined here vis-à-vis the teaching philosophy espoused in Chapter 1. Now it is appropriate to move on from this issue and consider one of the more controversial issues in EE, the business plan.

NOTES

1. See De Bono (1995) for a fuller discussion regarding the nature of developing creative ideas and, more importantly, selecting good ideas.
2. See Kim and Mauborgne (2000).
3. See Timmons (1999), specifically the discussion in Chapters 3 and 4 on idea evaluation.
4. See Choo (2006: 67).
5. See Bhaskar (1975).
6. See English and Moate (2009), also http://www.teaching-entrepreneurship.com/ideas.html.

10. Business Plans

Let me state from the outset, I do not apologise for allowing my personal biases against *traditional* business plans to shape the structure of this chapter. Indeed, I hope that such bias may restore some balance to the issue of *if* and *how* EE students should engage with business plans during their studies in higher education. Therefore, this chapter deliberately aims to be provocative in its consideration of the use of business plans in EE. However, the context of this discussion will tap into emergent discontent surrounding the issue that has been revealed in the IE Survey. This is a contemporary issue within EE and one that requires of each and every educator a considered position as to what approach is chosen. This chapter therefore aims to assist the reader to understand the respective arguments related to the topic and to also consider alternative approaches to the issue as well as providing an opportunity for the reader to reflect upon their personal position.

The chapter is structured as follows. First, the arguments for and against business plans as an educational tool will be considered. Then, several ontological issues will be considered with a view to suggesting an alternative approach to business planning in higher education, before an opportunity to reflect on the issues presented. But first let's briefly consider what a business plan is.

WHAT IS A BUSINESS PLAN?

Technically, the Collins English Dictionary[1] defines a business plan as: a detailed plan setting out the objectives of a business, the strategy and tactics planned to achieve them, and the expected profits, usually over a period of three to ten years. Alternatively, academically speaking,[2] it is considered to be: a document that articulates the critical aspects, basic assumptions and financial projections regarding a business venture. It is also the basic document used to interest and attract support, financial or otherwise, for a new business concept. In essence, it is what you intend to do, where you intend to do it, how you intend to do it, what resources (internal and external to you) will be required to do it, and what degree of sustainability and performance is expected.

I challenge you to now consider the pedagogical context of the business plan in higher education. Reintroducing the process of constructive alignment, let us again ask, what is a business plan? I would contend that it's not a learning outcome or a method of assessment; therefore it must be a *learning activity*. Why be so pedantic in locating the position of business plans in EE? Well, if we can agree that it is neither a learning outcome nor a method of assessment then we can logically accept that it should be informed by the development of directly related learning outcomes, and it should be instructive to the development of directly related methods of assessment. I am not convinced that such pedagogical soundness surrounds the current usage of business plans in EE.

Bill Bygrave recently noted[3] with reference to a quote attributed to Winston Churchill: 'However elegant the strategy, you should occasionally look at the results'. Bill suggested that if we substitute *business plan* for *strategy*, the quotation provides an apt summary of his advice to educators who place too much emphasis on teaching students how to write elegant business plans but seldom look at the outcome of their development in the real world. It's an interesting challenge to contemplate; however for now, let's consider the support for business plans in EE.

Support for Business Plans

Perhaps the easiest place to commence this discussion is by considering the support for business plans, because there seems to be lots of it. Dr Rob Fuller, Director of Entrepreneur Development Programs, Rady School of Management, University of California, San Diego, believes understanding the business planning *process* is a critical skill and tends to help students understand how to gather pertinent data and present it in a convincing manner. He further noted that learning to modify developing concepts based on evolving data are important skills to being an entrepreneur and/or an intrapreneur. In a similar vein, Professor Joseph Erba of the University of North Carolina in Greensboro, USA argues that the *process* of developing a business plan (if properly taught and managed) is a great learning tool regardless of whether the concept comes to fruition. Further, he contends, developing a solid business plan touches upon many basic but critically important elements and concepts of general business.

The essence of such commonly held views appears to rest on the assumption that we are teaching students a *process* that has a benefit to the future contexts our students have yet to encounter. I say commonly held views because the topic of business plans is a central element of seemingly every generalist text on entrepreneurship. Monica Kreuger, President of Global Infobrokers in Canada, strongly supports the process of going through the research and analysis, that writing a business plan is invaluable whether you start a business or not. She states that planning is part of the world of work and this is one type of plan; that writing a paper in another subject also seems silly but the process of organising thought, making a case and coming to a conclusion is used a million times in our lives; the final outcome of the plan is where students are often blown away by the physical results of their effort. She therefore believes it is vital to have this component to open the door to what might be and to give them the sense that they absolutely can do it. Such views are strongly supported throughout the responses in the IE Survey. However, I remain troubled by what seems to be the automatic inclusion of the business plan in EE.

Do we teach it for academic reasons, or is the (real world) role of the business plan in the financing process the driving factor? I am not sure which preceded the other, but it has become seemingly universally accepted. As hinted in previous chapter, I hold several reservations, but first let's get a sense of other concerns.

Business Plan Concerns

In recent times, Allan Gibb has frequently questioned the overt focus upon business plans within EE. One reason is that business plans can be created by highly formal and uninspiring efforts. As Bill Bygrave has noted, they may be elegant but what about the results? If we adopt the *they are learning a process* focus, such concerns may be lessened but, I would argue not eliminated. Let's dare to consider outcomes. A recent study[4] concluded that 'unless a would-be entrepreneur needs to raise substantial start-up capital from institutional investors or business angels, there is no compelling reason to write a detailed business plan before opening a new business'. If we accept the validity of this study, why are we teaching students how to write a business plan? I think this question can be answered in many different ways.

First, an observation that can be drawn from the IE Survey; EE students may be just as likely to be educated by an existing entrepreneur, as they are a past entrepreneur, as they are a non-entrepreneur. I hold no particular opinion as to what life experience any enterprise educator should possess. I have met brilliant educators in EE that have come from a wide variety of backgrounds.

Second, I feel it is only natural that some educators will approach their students' learning from a developmental approach, whereas others will fundamentally view education as a linear process. However, such differences matter in how we make sense of the potential value of business plans. To the former the value of a business plan is determined by the trajectory of each individual student. To the latter, the value of a business plan is its ability to combine their previous learning into one vehicle.

Third, whilst some may see enterprise on the whole as a rapidly escalating resource-hungry process, others conceive it to be a process that frequently starts without significant financial resources, evolving via constant feedback from the marketplace; feedback that may not be known accurately in advance. Clearly, it is not surprising there are differences of opinion.

Outright Rejection of the Business Plan

There are some educators who simply do not see value in having students complete a business plan. Professor Colin Gray from the Open University in the UK does not encourage the development of a business plan, instead developing a capacity to understand the analysis and decisions that underpin a good plan. I share Colin's confidence in this approach. I have successfully used a debating process within which students must adopt the position of business plan proponent or investor. Such a process is a sound way of allowing students to be exposed to multiple contexts around which business plans have been developed. Likewise, Professor Maurice Mulvenna at Ulster University in the UK argues that the business plan approach is a bit out of date, noting he would rather get the students to work in groups to explore a range of aspects for a business start-up. Philippe Sommer of the University of Virginia Darden School in the United States argues that writing plans is the last thing entrepreneurs do – *only* – when they need to raise money. *De-risking* a business is the first thing they do. Students are taught to write plans as an academic exercise, thus it is the wrong place to start. Further, he notes that the emphasis on plan writing tends to come from people who are educators and may not be entrepreneurs.

Clearly there are some passionate proponents on both sides of this debate. There are some interesting views expressed in the IE Survey that shine a little light on to how we came to such a contested outcome. Associate Professor Pi-Shen Seet of Flinders University in Australia senses that strategy educators have vacated the planning space, leaving it vacant and open to exploitation by authors of EE texts. This development, he argues, has implications for the type of skill set we offer to our students. I feel this makes sense, and it's interesting to see strategy, marketing, computing and engineering educators all pulling the business plan into their teaching space. I believe such encroachment into *our* space offers enterprise educators a unique opportunity to redefine the distinctiveness of our domain. Let's consider the nature of such opportunities by discussing some alternative approaches to business plans.

ALTERNATIVE APPROACHES

There is a clear paradox in my resistance to the universal development of business plans by my students. Overall, I am not against them, and I am not for them. Again, for me it is the actual needs of the student that must take precedent. Needs that cannot be known in advance of our meeting in our first class. Therefore, a simple alternative approach is to simply offer the students choice. If the pathway that lies before any particular student would be assisted or enlightened by the development of a business plan, then so be it. If however, there is no need for the student to construct a business plan, then why should they?

It is always interesting to ask educators the simple question whether they are able to teach in a manner that they choose. Invariably the answer is yes. However, just the slightest attempt at scratching the surface of their approach typically reveals many factors that restrict their ability to teach in a manner of their choosing. Within this first idea is the notion of curriculum flexibility, the idea that we can employ different learning activities and assessment procedures within a single class. Herein lies one of the hidden issues related to business plans in EE. The assumption that all students must partake learning activities in a consistent manner. This reduces the business plan issue to an all or nothing outcome. Why not ensure the curriculum respects the actual heterogeneous needs of our students?

ONTOLOGY AGAIN

In the previous chapter we considered the process of evaluating ideas and argued for the separation of idea evaluation and business planning. Let's return to where we left off so that we might consider another alternative form of business plan. The IDEAS process discussed earlier enables my students to develop judgement with respect to evaluating the commercial potential of an idea. The next challenge is to convert any such judgement into a business plan. What I will outline is not intended to meet the standard requirements of a traditional business plan. The aim is to transition the student from judgement to an evaluation of assumptions, to consideration of the questions that need answers, to finally framing an argument for value creation based on real answers.

Essentially, what I am suggesting is a plan derived from substance and not structured around a template. The IDEAS process contains 40 specific areas targeted for evaluation by personal judgement. I would simply contend that any business plan must account for four specific issues of concern and the nature of risk that relates to each of them. Employing this logic there are more than 160 questions that might arise from revisiting each of the 40 forms of personal judgement and their associated assumptions made within the IDEAS process.

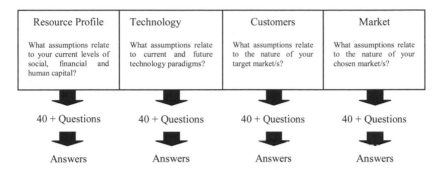

Figure 10.1 Judgements, assumptions, questions and answers

In Figure 10.1 the process of unpacking the judgements related to the IDEAS process is illustrated. Revisiting each of the individual judgements in the context of the four specific issues noted above allows the student to embed into their thinking *risk* across every aspect of their planning. I argue this is critically important to developing a plan that closes the distance between reality and fanciful thinking. What I am proposing is a way of thinking based on substance and not structured around any pre-determined template. An approach that accounts for the spatial and temporal separation between the student's idea and the expected reality it is assumed to relate to. So, our students move from a range of personal judgements to a consideration of the assumptions that must exist for such judgements to have been formed. Assumptions that can be connected to each of the four specific issues illustrated in Figure 10.1. From this process, multiple questions will naturally arise, questions that represent the process of completing the due diligence of an idea.

However, it is how we ask the questions that determines the nature of the answers acquired. Starting from each assumption, the student is able to ask (with reference to each of the four specific issues) under what conditions would their assumptions hold; conversely, under what conditions would their assumptions not hold? Through this process risk is not used within the last hour of planning to provide reassurance of the plan's underlying logic; it is used to create the underlying logic for the translation of the idea into a start-up. Thus, the students' confidence is developed through knowing, not from guessing and/or assuming. The next idea is to go beyond the idea of a business plan to that of an implementation plan.

Implementation Plans

Bill Bygrave[4] and colleagues at Babson College offer some interesting insights into this discussion that predate the development of the discussion. Reflecting upon business plan competitions at Babson, they draw a neat analogy between what is rewarded by athletic departments and what is increasingly rewarded in entrepreneurship classes. Athletic departments, they argue, reward success, not play-book competitions. What, they ask, is the logic of rewarding students for writing intellectual plans and presenting them stylishly, rather than for implementing actual businesses? It is a good question and one that is beholden upon all educators in our field to ask themselves. They further argue that entrepreneurship, just like football, is a contact sport and not merely a classroom intellectual exercise. So, it's about focus; an immediate focus upon what must be done to start up. Not grandiose expositions of what will happen if all of the ducks mysteriously align.

I am drawn to the logic of their arguments; why are we assessing proposals for possible future success when we cannot actually know if the idea contained within the plan would indeed succeed? Perhaps the future of EE needs to be aligned to assessing actual implementation of enterprising behaviour. This is very consistent with the emerging 4Cs approach at UTAS where it is the process and outcomes that by and large are assessed rather than interim artefacts of the students' thinking. The next alternative approach is upon developing a capacity within our students for engineering the lean start-up. I would argue that it converts the logic of the implementation plan from thinking to doing, reflecting and then doing more.

The Lean Start-Up

The lean start-up methodology pioneered by Eric Ries[5] has captured the interest of many folks interested in the *process* of start-ups. The approach is premised upon the notion that we waste too much effort on developing products that have little market fit, thereby reducing the prospects of surviving the start-up phase. So rather than doing a written plan, our students could be living their actual plan through testing their ideas earlier than normal, working closely with customers and gaining instant feedback. Thus, an approach through which idea failure doesn't have to mean company failure. In essence, there is no building a company around an optimistic vision, because it is the elements of the vision that are tested directly with your assumed customers.

The lean start-up methodology also provides a different kind of focus for our students. The aim is to start your interaction with customers on the underlying core product or service, not contemplate the accumulation of every conceivable feature so as to secure a contestable market niche. The aim is to learn early, to learn often. By using a minimal offering our students have all that is necessary to commence a genuine conversation with the target market. They can build in the required features as they engage with their customers. So let us recap the ideas presented thus far.

There are two clear schools of thought regarding the use of business plans for EE students in higher education. The majority I suspect support them either as a mechanism for gaining funding or as a means of organising one's thoughts and learning how to plan. Conversely, a (growing) minority of educators I suspect see little value in having EE students complete a business plan. Whilst I tend to side with the minority, I do not see the debate as involving diametrically opposite arguments. Again, it is the dialogic relations that exist separately across institutions that matter. The challenge it would seem is to ensure that the process is not merely template driven on the assumed need of venture capital or angel investment. Whatever format is offered should be idea dependent, and most importantly, it should be reality dependent because this is where the greatest learning opportunities are. The lean start-up approach I would argue is a process of planning-as-practice not practise-of-planning. So, the questions that remain fall to you to consider.

DETERMINING THE LOGIC OF YOUR APPROACH

As always, your teaching philosophy needs influence your actions in this regard. How you believe your students learn; what you believe they should learn; what the impact of such learning should be; what activities they should engage with to learn; what type of learning environment is required to facilitate the delivery of such learning activities; and how you will assess the nature of their learning. Returning to these fundamental questions will enable you to find the answers that guide your usage of business plans and/or alternative approaches in your curriculum. The key questions are always yours and no one else's. My only advice to you is that you consider the diversity of needs and aspirations in each student cohort you encounter. Think about how you can facilitate choice for your students. To the extent that we as educators can incorporate choice into our students' curriculum we can avoid much of the either/or nature of the debate that currently surrounds the use of business plans in EE. Ultimately, your approach to this issue should be determined more by your understanding of your teaching philosophy than by the nature of debate that surrounds this issue. Because from that approach, you will also be capable of defending the logic of your approach vis-à-vis the learning needs of your students.

NOTES

1. See Collins English Dictionary (2009).
2. See Stevenson et al. (1999: 43).
3. I have gained a more grounded perspective on the value of business plans and their role in higher education from my discussion with Bill Bygrave (2010).
4. See Lange et al. (2007).
5. See http://www.startuplessonslearned.com/ and http://www.socrated.com/user_courses/226 for excellent sources of information on the lean start-up process.

PART IV

Towards an Ecology of Learning

11. Accounting for Interaction

The aim of this final chapter is to unite the various ideas previously presented into a coherent explanation of teaching entrepreneurship in higher education. Throughout this book, frequent references have been made to ecological and/or evolutionary concepts and theories. Therefore, before we progress any further I will take some time to explain how such ideas when united allow us to understand the complexity that forever surrounds us.

The fundamental task of any *ecological* approach is to 'delineate the general principles under which the natural community [under investigation] and ... its component parts operate'.[1] This entails accounting for all interacting entities occurring within a specific area and understanding the coactions between each and the relations they experience with their environs. Such an approach is *evolutionary* to the extent that it also seeks to explain events occurring over time with reference to mechanisms of selection that act upon all manner of variations, some of which are retained during the entity's struggle to survive. I believe that this minimal benchmark sets at least an equivalent standard to that previously used to consider the interaction between students and the higher education environments they encounter.[2] The primary difference here is that the educator is elevated to the same status as the students in terms of interacting within the campus environment. Thus, unlike approaches centred on the development of the student, my approach captures the primary dialogic relationship between the educator and the student, whilst considering the nature of the environment within which their interaction occurs.

ONE LAST BIG IDEA

To advance my aims in this chapter I need to introduce one last idea, which introduces a framework which the remainder of the discussion can be referenced to. As I have previously discussed elsewhere,[3] this idea was first outlined by Edward Haskell[4] as coaction theory. Coaction theory is used to separate diversely powerful individuals into the *weak* and the *strong*; in this case, students and educators. Haskell argued that weak and strong individuals have nine, and only nine, qualitatively different (coaction) relations to each other. In Figure 11.1 below, an adaptation of Haskell's clarification scheme is illustrated.

0 Indicates neutral interaction outcomes
\+ Indicates positive interaction outcomes
– Indicates neutral interaction outcomes

LECTURER \ STUDENT	–	0	+
+	– + Predation	0 + Allotrophy	+ + Symbiosis
0	– 0 Amensalism	0 0 Neutrality	+ 0 Commensalism
–	– – Synnecrosis	0 – Allolimy	+ – Parasitism

Adapted from: Haskell (1949)

Figure 11.1 An adaptation of Haskell's coaction theory

In Figure 11.1 nine forms of coaction are illustrated for both the lecturer and/or student. Note that the only type of interaction between lecturer and student that is mutually beneficial is symbiosis (+ +). Within commensalism (+ 0), the student gains from the interaction and the lecturer is unaffected by the experience. So by and large, there are more forms of coaction related to sub-optimal outcomes for the student than there are acceptable positive outcomes. The value of enlisting coaction theory should be obvious. We as educators must understand the nature of interaction that relates to positive outcomes for students and educators alike. In doing so, we must be prepared to accept that some of our students may be negatively impacted by the learning processes they experience. Clearly there is a challenge for us all in addressing this dilemma. However, to the extent that we cannot appreciate how we and our students are impacted by our coactions we are simply hoping that everything will be alright. The remainder of this chapter now seeks to bring together the ideas within this book so that you can reflectively imagine a pathway forward that is beneficial for you and your students.

IMAGINING A NEW WORLD

On the basis that you can accept that not *everything* in your teaching world is perfect, we have some space to imagine an improved world. The aim of our musings should be to establish symbiotic coactions with all stakeholders, but most importantly between the educator and the students. We can live with not everything being perfect if the nature of coaction between educator and student is positive for both parties. The challenge of this task is daunting; to account for the nature of all relevant interactions requires a high degree of skill. There will always be a lot of temporal arguments through this type of process as to which element precedes the other, but let's try not to allow this issue to sidetrack us. To the extent that you are able to *think* about all of the ideas that have preceded this chapter, within this chapter, you have already developed a capacity to *think about how to teach EE*, and that is the fundamental aim of this book. My challenge to you is to contextualise the ideas and their integration that follow into the world you live in.

The world that is yours to imagine will have many similarities to most EE educators the world over; however it is how the pieces of your EE jigsaw fit together that matter. That is why developing a capacity to think about how to teach EE is so important. It is dissimilarities that matter, and it's your job to understand why. Therefore, I invite you to take up the challenge to sense the invisible forces that exist (regardless of our awareness) through which our students' learning outcomes are so indelibly determined; forces that can be imagined, harnessed and manipulated by the *thinking* and ever-reflective educator.

YOUR JIGSAW PIECES

If we return to the ideas that have been offered to you for consideration throughout this book, you have the pieces of your own EE jigsaw. I have consistently argued for the importance of your teaching philosophy. Without an awareness of your teaching philosophy you are effectively a rudderless ship directed by external forces. An awareness of your teaching philosophy does not grant you control over your journeys, but better prepares you to be able to navigate the expected challenges you will confront.

Next, I would argue you need to have in mind an imagined set of learning outcomes. What is it your students will be capable of upon graduation? I argue that in overloading students with content we assume they will need one day we are in fact depriving our students of a true opportunity to become enterprising in their here and now. I have offered you the notion of the reasonable adventurer as an example of where my focus is in this regard. A student becomes a reasonable adventurer on the basis they can create their own opportunities for satisfaction in life; they do this through developing personal skills related to six specific attributes. Thus my curriculum is built around the presence of six attributes that enable my students to learn *for* and *through* enterprise. Where is your focus? What is at the heart of your teaching philosophy that you will attempt to translate into elements of an achievable curriculum?

A recognisable process that you can confidently trust to guide this process is that of constructive alignment. Again, it is a matter of asking what my students need to learn. What learning activities would best enable my students to achieve the desired learning outcomes? And, what forms of assessment would allow me to know if the students have achieved the intended learning requirements? There are many ways this process can be derailed. Maybe you will not truly determine what your students need to learn with enough precision. Perhaps you will not be able to conceive or deliver the types of learning activities that would be required to facilitate such learning. The key here is to remain very aware of what is happening globally in this regard, to understand the nature of student diversity you will encounter, and to also understand what represents legitimate practice at your institution.

As more pieces are added to our jigsaw, more assumptions are being created as well. Let us pause a moment to consider those that emerge in the above passage. There is an assumption present that you have the capacity to be highly reflective. Are you? How often do you consult with your colleagues, your students, the literature and most importantly, yourself, on matters relating to teaching and learning? How adventurous are you when it comes to adding and deleting aspects of your curriculum? How often do your submit papers to conferences and journal publications based on some degree of reflection of your teaching practice?

The diversity of your student cohorts is a piece of the jigsaw that is difficult to incorporate. However, without its inclusion the final picture will be distorted. Bringing the elephant in the room to life adds both levels of complexity and opportunities to enable learning to occur. The capacity for our students to reflect is greatly enhanced through their awareness and acceptance of the student diversity they contribute to.

Clearly there are assumptions we must make as to your ability to navigate the legitimacy landscape at your institution; a landscape that will undoubtedly vary from one institution to the next. Landscape is a useful term as the terrain can be steep to climb with certain traditions favoured over others. Alternatively, sometimes we are left on our own to plot the way through a largely virgin area. Frequently, we experience a combination of open and closed spaces within which to teach. Just as entrepreneurs must cope with factors that may or may not favour them, every EE educator must be prepared to advance the needs of their students, even when that means circumventing those factors that do not support curriculum initiatives designed to aid your students' learning.

THEIR JIGSAW PIECES

Your students control several pieces of the eventual jigsaw as well; pieces that you alone cannot place into the puzzle without their say so. We cannot predict or force our students' learning, a critically important point related to the ontological aspects of EE discussed in Chapter 3. The transformational aspects of EE require of each educator to ensure each student has the opportunity to reflect upon their learning journey. The key issue therefore is to comprehend the divergent nature of each student's journey. Unlike many content-driven subjects, EE should enable each student to explicitly travel a personal journey. In a sense, we as educators should co-create a different jigsaw puzzle with every student. They will develop personally at different rates and different directions with different ideas. Therefore, how could it be any other way?

The resource profile of each student relative to the ideas of their mind represents jigsaw pieces that are subject to change at a moment's whim. If the student changes their idea, they will almost certainly change the nature of their resource profile. Thus, our students' pieces of the puzzle are less certain, as is their placement in the puzzle. The skill of the EE educator is a capacity to suspend judgement as to what the puzzle will resemble whilst each student's deliberations are subject to change. Whilst the pieces of the potential puzzle are tenuous, the emerging enterprising mindset of each student should not be. The capacity of each student to understand their ability to engage in enterprising behaviour should be incrementally developing across the course of their studies. Thus, their individual mindsets have the potential to organise the configuration of any puzzle.

Likewise, the students' skill set is an important piece of the puzzle that is constantly evolving during the term of their studies. They represent enabling qualities that can act as the glue that holds the eventual puzzle together. It is intertwined with the development of the student's mindset. It is critical that our students are afforded sufficient space to observe this developmental process. I have discussed at length the importance of reflection. It is through reflective behaviour that our students can stand back and smell the roses. Thus far we have discussed the pieces of the jigsaw puzzle that the educator and student both bring to the table. What about the other pieces that all too often are seemingly invisible?

THE TRICKY JIGSAW PIECES

The learning environment holds the other vital pieces to the puzzle. The atmosphere that is created, shared and supported will aid or diminish our efforts to create enterprising students. In Chapter 3 the notion of relational trust was briefly discussed. It was argued that the presence of relational trust provides a means for the educator, the students and the learning environment they co-create to be altered continuously through mutual understanding and respect. I would contend that symbiotic or at least commensalistic relationships are possible only because of the creation of relational trust. Any other form of coaction will of course lead to negative long-term outcomes.

The big question that arises relates to the extent that you are working *on* rather than merely *in* the learning environment. Collectively, there are many jigsaw pieces floating around at any one time, all belonging to different jigsaw puzzles. Sounds rather chaotic doesn't it? That's because it is, that is the nature of EE, or at least it should be. In Chapter 1 I stated that, *I have always felt that entrepreneurial learning is not related to memorising external bodies of knowledge, but rather it is about self-recognition of internal knowledge. It is not always about events that are planned or predictable, but frequently about unplanned and unpredictable events. It is less about the knowledge of the educator, and more about the support of the educator. It is about the creation of what doesn't exist, rather than the maintenance of that which does. It is about freedom, not restriction, and it is as much about failure as it is success.* Cast your mind back to your various attempts to complete a jigsaw puzzle. Frequently, we rely upon trial and error processes to complete the task. We cannot know in advance the order of how the pieces will fit together, all we can have faith in is that they will eventually fit together. This is our challenge as EE educators; to be patient and supportive of those that seek to find order in the chaos. Just as we cannot force a child to complete their complex jigsaw challenge, we must also be able to allow our students to find their way forward. That they may give up and not return to the challenge is not the end of the world. The key is ensuring they understand where they are placed relative to the challenge. This is the value of reflection.

THE UNIQUENESS OF OUR VIEW

There is uniqueness to our view of the world on every matter we encounter. Our challenge as EE educators is to strengthen and connect our students' reflective capacities to the lives they live within our classrooms. On the front cover of this book is an image chosen specifically to capture the nature of the challenge we as EE educators face daily. That we can open the door to the cage that has held our students captive throughout their schooling does not mean they are ready to fly. For all the reasons discussed throughout this book, many of our students simply do not have the resource profile to take flight. There should be no shame in any such inaction. What is important is that our students can appreciate and understand the view afforded to them from being outside the cage rather than confined inside.

Developing the reflective student creates the capacity for greater and surer choice. The temptation to leap into a new venture is replaced with the calmness of knowing what is missing vis-à-vis social, human and financial capital. What is critical is ensuring that each student has had the opportunity to experience success and failure within the boundaries of your curriculum. That they have learnt about their capacity to be enterprising and manage relationships, risk and their fleeting aspirations. I say fleeting because our students should be encouraged to play with as many ideas as possible.

A challenge we as educators share with our students is that of the limitations and/or richness of our world view. We must be mindful of the degree to which our collective minds are in or out of sync. First, we may have little experience and/or insight into the world our students wish to create/enter. In this instance we must be careful to not to allow our ignorance get in the way of their imagination. Our challenge is to ensure that we evoke the ontological necessity of asking our students to explain the conditions under which such value can be created and captured. Second, we may have intimate knowledge of the domain our students wish to enter. We may be capable of raining on their parade without them understanding our failure to support their enthusiasm. Either way, we must be mindful of the competing visions we are surrounded with in the presence of our students, we must be patient in sharing our judgement. We must however ensure reality looms large.

No Room for the Myths

As the pieces of the jigsaw puzzle fly about chaotically, we must ensure that many of the entrepreneurship myths are debunked so as not to allow any false sense of reality to take grip. My good friend Barry Moltz[5] details the pitfalls of being an entrepreneur exquisitely in his first book, *You Need to be a Little*

Crazy: The Truth about Starting and Growing Your Business. Put simply, being in business for yourself can make you sick. It can rip apart the nature of your most valued personal relationships. It can send you spiralling into a state of depression. Many of us have experienced the dark side of the *freedom* of entrepreneurship. We must ensure our students understand when the puzzle is for play and when it is for real. When are the pieces being played with and when do we expect them to leave them in place for others to judge their collective fit?

Most texts on entrepreneurship discuss the issue of the entrepreneur's need for a locus of control or increasingly now their ability to effectuate; I believe that we must be careful with such concepts. Notions of freedom are commonly placed alongside the motives of entrepreneurs and their future-oriented actions. I have met few entrepreneurs who claim to be free. I would ask you to consider what is freedom in the context of entrepreneurship?

If it is the emancipation of time and/or dependence upon customers and debtors, then freedom is not always much fun. Indeed, there is a need to ensure the developing enterprise mindset is forged through exposure to actual pressures through which such freedom is explored. It is critically important that such development does not lead to over-confidence or hubris. The combination of failure and reflection provides a potent force to shape our students. To shield them from the opportunity to fail and recover is to severely limit their capacity for personal development.

CONNECTING THE PIECES

Hopefully you have noticed the almost complete absence of consideration given to what topics our students should or could learn. The aim, as stated from the beginning, was to create a reflective space for you to contemplate *thinking about teaching entrepreneurship*. Not *what* or *how* to teach entrepreneurship. As we draw towards the end of this process, I hope you have considered the consequences of finding the swirling pieces of all the jigsaw puzzles revolving around you. Some of the pieces are of your making, some are not. Some can be controlled by you, others at best, directed by you. And yet, you are the most powerful person in the room, when you are the least visible person in the room. This is the secret to working *on* rather than merely *in* the learning environment. When we seek to control the learning environment, connecting the pieces is not possible. There are simply too many permutations possible for any one person to do so. We must let our students succeed or fail in creating their ever-changing puzzle. So how can we earn our pay as invisible folk I hear you ask?

Mentor your students when they ask for help. Become the silent partner in their adventures. Allow them the opportunity to connect their concrete experiences via observations, reflections and the formation of abstract thinking to new solutions for their recognisable problems and opportunities. In doing so, you will allow them to learn from within, rather than merely from outside. Let us conclude by contemplating one final set of questions about your approach.

Thinking About EE

We started with the most important issue of all: your teaching philosophy. Without a teaching philosophy you are naked for all the wrong reasons. A well-developed teaching philosophy represents the emperor's clothes in the true traditions of the old tale. Without it you are naked to all, with it shared and understood you will be admired for your convictions and intent. So, several essential questions await your immediate attention; how you believe your students learn; what you believe they should learn; what should be the impact of such learning; what activities they should engage with to learn; what type of learning environment is required to facilitate the delivery of such learning activities; how you will assess the nature of their learning; and how you will implement and monitor/adjust your teaching philosophy.

In the absence of progress in this regard, may I suggest that you start to engage in conversations with other EE educators. We are all faced with similar challenges and I find talking such issues through with other EE folk helps bring clarity to my own thinking. Along the way you must be able to navigate expected issues of legitimacy related to the context of your teaching. A range of dialogic relationships that facilitate interaction between all stakeholders will inevitably shape the evolutionary trajectory of your teaching's development. Can you map the nature of these relationships and how you will manage such interactions?

Defining EE

Within the world you share with your students, how will you define EE? Clearly your determination of the role and of EE should be partly derived from your teaching philosophy. To not do so would be to outsource the task to others who are quite likely to be disconnected from the situation of your teaching. My own biases towards the personal development of my students have delivered me to a position of saying that EE is *a process of transformational education through which students are encouraged to better understand their capacity to create future opportunities for satisfaction through exposure to different learning experiences crafted from a learner-*

centred approach. So, taking into account your philosophical approach, your institutional issues, the nature of your students and their aspirations, how will you define EE in your local context?

VISUALISING YOUR GRADUATES

If another educator was to ask you to describe in detail the abilities of your graduates, what would you say? Would you be able to satisfy the demands of such a request? I have shared with you my notion of the reasonable adventurer, a graduate capable of creating their own opportunities for satisfaction. I have shared with you the six attributes of the reasonable adventurer. Hopefully I have demonstrated my conviction to help my students develop in a particular manner. A manner that I have argued is well suited to the unknown requirements of an enterprising life.

Much has been made of the importance of the process of constructive alignment throughout this book. It is offered to you as a robust tool that can help guide your planning in this regard. Defining the nature of your graduate stands you next to the nature of the learning outcomes you believe are of most importance to your students. Stepping back from a universal outcome of business start-up upon graduation, your deliberations need to align to the type of learning activities required to facilitate the students' learning. Activities that expose and prepare your students for a world of unknown opportunities. The key assumption here is that you understand how your students learn, all of them. Do you? To the extent that you cannot explain to someone else how your students learn, you still have more work to do on your teaching philosophy. Fear not, to question is to grow, it is how we make sense of the responsibilities we as EE educators have; responsibilities that are merely opportunities to excel and aid the transformation of students' lives.

HAIL THE ELEPHANT

A fundamental prerequisite of adopting an ecological approach is to be able to account for all the types of interacting elements. Our students do differ in important ways and we must understand and appreciate how. How will you construct your learning outcomes to accommodate the varied aspirations that reside in your classroom? How will you develop your learning activities to ensure sufficient choice is built in to enable individual students to engage in a meaningful way? How will you identify and measure the ever-present diversity in your classes? Most importantly, how will you use the presence of diversity to increase the capacity of your students to learn about themselves and the world they live in? We are all surrounded by a wonderful opportunity to amplify the power of our teaching through the inclusion of student diversity. Will you take advantage of this opportunity?

AT HOME IN THE LEARNING ENVIRONMENT

The old saying *the more things change the more they stay the same* is quite apt when contemplating the environs we share with our students. How do you explain the influence of your students' feedback on your future actions as an educator? How does your mutual engagement alter the atmosphere and general dynamics of your teaching and their learning? To what extent are they teaching you and you are learning from them? To what extent are you comfortable allowing the parameters of your learning space and related learning activities to shift under the weight of welcomed feedback?

We can learn to become one with the nature of ever-shifting parameters if we share the nature of any such process with our students and other colleagues. Yes, students look for stability in their environs, but let's not pretend we can always know perfectly in advance what is required. Just accepting the presence of an unknown quantity of student diversity in our environs creates pressures for readjustment. It can be an exciting process to share with others or a painful process to hold close to our chest. Will you take the time to contemplate the nature of change occurring in your environs? To be honest, if you aspire to be a quality educator, you have little choice. Accepting the transformational qualities of EE requires of you to accept that you will be meeting a slightly new cohort of students each class. Perhaps they are more confident, perhaps they have developed stronger friendships, or perhaps they have simply developed a greater capacity to question the veracity of the knowledge on offer. However they may have changed, the key is that they have changed. As a result your learning environs have been altered by their presence. I have introduced you to the process of niche construction to provide you with the means to understand how you can explain the process of any such change. The question that remains is how comfortable will you choose to become surrounded by ever-present change?

THE INTANGIBILITY OF OUR STUDENTS' PROMISE

Do we create graduates capable of tackling all manner of opportunities, or is their potential contextual? I have argued that it is largely contextual. That every student (or group of students) holds a particular resource profile vis-à-vis a particular opportunity. To what extent do you enable your students to match up the reality of their abilities to the requirements of their dreams? To what extent do you create opportunities for your students to improve the nature of their resource profile (relative to an opportunity), or retrofit their abilities to a more suitable opportunity? To what extent do you allow students the opportunity to succeed and/or fail and afford them the opportunity to use their resource profiles as a sense-making tool? To what extent do you enable your students to repeatedly succeed and/or fail so that the importance of their resource profile within different contexts can be tested?

This is the essence of learning *through* and *for* enterprise. It is the essence of learning from within one's personal experiences. Do you afford sufficient opportunity to reflect upon the degree to which their success and/or failure is largely predetermined by the personal (and group) qualities they hold relative to a specific opportunity? To what extent do you encourage and/or facilitate access to a range of mentors? Ensuring our students gain access to multiple honest perspectives is central to their ability to take responsibility for their learning. We cannot allow *teachable moments* to slide by, we must attempt to capture as many as possible so that our students can internalise them.

WE ARE WHO WE SELL

There would seem to be a growing acceptance that developing an ability to sell is of fundamental importance to EE students. How do you help your students to sense and respond to pain in society? How for that matter do your students learn about their own personality? How do they learn about their ability to interact effectively with all manner of folk they encounter? We can learn how to sell and selling should feature within the list of our students' learning outcomes.

I have offered a simple (some would say crude) approach to learning about personalities and selling for your consideration. It is by no means argued to be the best approach. It is simply an approach I favour; what approach would work for you and your students? What learning activities have you (or could be) developed to enable your students to develop and apply such valuable self-knowledge? Again, it is important to return to the roots of your teaching philosophy to ensure your thinking in this area is in accord with your other efforts. We can no longer afford to allow selling to be seen as the poor cousin of marketing. They are different things and should both be treated with the respect they equally deserve.

SORTING THE CHAFF FROM THE WHEAT

One of the most significant challenges that your students confront is deciding which ideas to commit their time and effort to exploring. I say significant because choosing the wrong ideas is quite likely to result in time being wasted, time that cannot be clawed back. As an educator it is so important that you ensure that your students understand the consequences of the choices they make in selecting a particular idea.

I have argued that we must ensure the processes of idea selection and due diligence are deliberately separated. We must ensure students understand why they are assessing an idea. Is it a comparative process, or is it to determine initial viability? The issue that must be addressed by you as an educator is the ability of your students to assess an idea that they are temporally or spatially separated from. Sometimes your students can work with no more than their personal judgement rather than rational facts. Is a one shot process for your students, or is it a process repeated to ensure familiarity with the process? Clearly there is a need for careful consideration of the ramifications of assuming students are always capable of assessing all manner of ideas. Indeed, we should exert much care to ensure our students understand the limitations they have when assessing an idea. We should not fall into the trap of allowing them to conclude they have successfully completed a task they may be incapable of doing diligently. The last issue for us to consider is that of the business plan.

TO PLAN OR NOT TO PLAN?

My biases with regards to having students complete a traditional business plan have been previously discussed. In reality my position is irrelevant, what is important is what you think. What do you believe, how did you reach this position, and how does this position play out relative to your teaching philosophy? Will your students all be seeking finance? Will they simply learn something valuable from completing the process? Essentially, what is your pedagogical logic for using business plans to advance your students' learning? Perhaps most importantly, how does your approach to this issue play out across each cohort vis-à-vis the ever-present student diversity? How might you be able to inject choice into your approach to increase the depth of learning opportunities for each student?

OVER TO YOU

Ultimately, teaching EE in higher education is a challenge. That's what makes it so much fun. Knowing there is no one way, but rather several justifiable ways to approach any issue is comforting. However, you will only be able to seek comfort from this fact if you have prepared a justification to your approach. That is where your teaching philosophy will provide you with a treasure trove of common sense to draw upon. I hope you have found space throughout this book to reflect on your approach. I hope that you feel inclined to continue this thinking. Whatever the outcome of your thinking, I wish you and your students the best of luck in your exploration of the unknown.

NOTES

1. See Clarke (1967: 18) to gain an appreciation of the true nature of the applied meaning of ecology.
2. The work of Banning (1978) represents the commencement of the notion of campus ecology. Whilst the ideas remain undeveloped in mainstream thinking, they nevertheless are thought provoking.
3. See Jones (2010b).
4. The original work of Haskell (1949) in identifying the nature of possible interactions between weak and strong entities has stood the test of time. The identified coactions remain as fundamentally important to ecology today as they originally did.
5. See Moltz (2003) for a truly thought provoking and honest assessment of the challenges of stepping out alone as an entrepreneur.

Appendices

APPENDIX 1: INTERNATIONAL EDUCATORS SURVEY

From December 2009 to May 2010 an online survey was distributed to educators known to the author and others holding membership at the online entrepreneurship education portal, www.entrepreneurshipandeducation.com. In total, 97 responses from 35 countries were received. The breakdown of the response was as follows: Australia (10 responses), Austria (1), Bhutan (1), Canada (2), China (1), Dominican Republic (1), Egypt (1), England (12), Finland (1), France (1), Germany (4), Hungary (1), India (1), Ireland (5), Kenya (1), Lithuania (1), Malaysia (2), Netherlands (1), New Zealand (3), Nigeria (2), Northern Ireland (1), Norway (2), Portugal (1), Puerto Rico (3), Saudi Arabia (2), Scotland (1), Serbia (1), Singapore (2), South Africa (3), Spain (1), Switzerland (1), Tanzania (1), Uganda (1), United States (23) and Wales (2).

General Characteristics of the Respondents

With regards to teaching experience, 25.5% of the respondents taught only at the level of undergraduate, the remainder taught both undergraduates and postgraduates. The vast majority of the respondents had been teaching entrepreneurship for more than five years (61.9%), with 26.8% having more than three years' experience but less than five years' experience, and 10.3% having more than one year's experience, but less than three years' experience. Only one respondent had less than one year's experience.

The vast majority of the respondents (77.3%) were classed as full-time academics, with the remainder part-time academics (14.4%), entrepreneurs in residence (3.1%) or invited lecturers (5.2%). In terms of entrepreneurial experience, 25.8% claimed to have previous experience and 21.6% stated they currently were practising entrepreneurs.

APPENDIX 2: PEDAGOGIES FOR TEACHING ENTREPRENEURSHIP

The National Council for Graduate Entrepreneurship (NCGE) in the UK has developed a compendium of pedagogies for teaching entrepreneurship that is developed around the identification of eight proposed target outcomes from entrepreneurial learning (see http://www.ncge.com).

Learning Outcomes Framework

1. Key entrepreneurial behaviours, skills and attitudes have been developed

2. Students clearly empathise with, understand and 'feel' the life-world of the entrepreneur

3. Key entrepreneurial values have been inculcated

4. Motivation towards a career in entrepreneurship has been built and students clearly understand the comparative benefits

5. The students understand the process (stages) of going into business, the associated tasks and learning needs

6. Students have the generic competencies associated with entrepreneurship

7. Students have a grasp of key business how to's associated with the start-up process

8. Students understand the nature of the relationships they need to develop with key stakeholders and are familiarised with them

In turn each of the eight proposed outcomes can be expanded upon to provide general instruction to aid their inclusion into a specific curriculum. Specifically, this process draws attention to:

- Entrepreneurial behaviours, skills and attributes including emotional intelligence
- Preparation for the 'way of life' of the entrepreneur

- Entrepreneurial values and ways of doing things, feeling things, organising things, communicating things and learning things experientially
- Entrepreneurial behaviour and management in different contexts – not just business
- Ideas harvesting, grasping and realisation of opportunity
- Managing entrepreneurially, holistically and strategically (know how)
- Managing and learning from relationships (know who)

Entrepreneurial Learning Outcomes

1. Entrepreneurial behaviour, attitude and skill development	
Key entrepreneurial behaviours, skills and attitudes have been developed (these will need to be agreed and clearly set out)	To what degree does a programme have activities that seek clearly to develop: • opportunity seeking • initiative taking • ownership of a development • commitment to see things through • personal locus of control (autonomy) • intuitive decision making with limited information • networking capacity • strategic thinking • negotiation capacity • selling/persuasive capacity • achievement orientation • incremental risk taking

2. Creating empathy with the entrepreneurial life world	
Students clearly empathise with, understand and 'feel' the life-world of the entrepreneur	To what degree does the programme help students to 'feel' the world of: • living with uncertainty and complexity • having to do everything under pressure • coping with loneliness • holistic management • no sell, no income • no cash in hand, no income • building know who and trust relationships • learning by doing, copying, making things up, problem solving • managing interdependencies • working flexibly and long hours

3. Key entrepreneurial values	
Key entrepreneurial values have been inculcated	To what degree does the programme seek to inculcate and create empathy with key entrepreneurial values: • strong sense of independence • distrust of bureaucracy and its values • self made/self belief • strong sense of ownership • belief that rewards come with own effort • 'hard work brings its rewards' • believe can make things happen • strong action orientation • belief in informal arrangements • strong belief in the value of know who and trust • strong belief in freedom to take action • belief in the individual and community not the state

4. Motivation to entrepreneurship career	
Motivation towards a career in entrepreneurship has been built and students clearly understand the comparative benefits	To what degree does the programme help students to: • understand the benefits from an entrepreneurship career • compare with employee career • have some entrepreneurial 'hero's' as friends & acquaintances • have images of entrepreneurial people 'just like them'

5. Understanding of processes of business entry and tasks	
Students understand the process (stages) of setting up an organisation, and the associated tasks and learning needs	To what degree does the programme take students through: • the total process of setting up an organisation from idea to survival and provide understanding of what challenges will arise at each stage • helping students learn how to handle them

6. Generic entrepreneurship competencies	
Students have the key generic competencies associated with entrepreneurship (generic 'how to's')	To what degree does the programme build the capacity to: • find an idea • appraise an idea • see problems as opportunities • identify the key people to be influenced in any development • build the know who • learn from relationships • assess business development needs • know where to look for answers • improve emotional self awareness, manage and read emotions and handle relationships • constantly see yourself and the business through the eyes of stakeholders and particularly customers

7. Key minimum business how to's	
Students have a grasp of key business how to's associated with the start up process	To what degree does the programme help students to: • see products and services as combinations of benefits • develop a total service package • price a product service • identify and approach good customers • appraise and learn from competition • monitor the environment with limited resources • choose appropriate sales strategy and manage it • identify the appropriate scale of a business to make a living • set standards for operations performance and manage them • finance the business appropriately from different sources • develop a business plan as a relationship communication instrument • acquire an appropriate system to manage cash, payments, collections, profits and costs • select a good accountant • manage, with minimum fuss, statutory requirements

8. Managing relationships	
Students understand the nature of the relationships they need to develop with key stakeholders and are familiarised with them	How does the programme help students to: • identify all key stakeholders impacting upon any venture • understand the needs of all key stakeholders at the start up and survival stage • know how to educate stakeholders • know how to learn from them • know how best to build and manage the relationship

The above illustrated learning outcomes have been designed to truly represent achievable outcomes, not inputs. During the process of identifying the types of pedagogies currently used to teach entrepreneurship and developing a guide to assist educators, the NCGE has also mapped each of the pedagogies to the above noted learning outcomes. Note, it is not suggested that there are only 44 possible pedagogies; the process of identification and mapping continues on, potentially forever.

Teaching Pedagogies Identified for Teaching Entrepreneurship

1. Small group teaching
2. Entrepreneurial facilitation
3. Use of ice breakers
4. Use of external speakers/presenters or evaluators
5. Use of drama
6. Use of debate
7. Use of drawing
8. Use of hot seats
9. Speed-networking
10. Use of an elevator pitch
11. Use of revolving tables
12. Use of brainstorming using post-its
13. Use of panels
14. Use of critical incidents
15. Use of organisations as networks
16. Use of empathy in communication exercises (with entrepreneurs)
17. Use of shadowing
18. Use of role play
19. Use of frames of reference for intuitive decision making
20. Use of psychometric tests
21. Use of locus of control tests
22. Use of relationship learning
23. Use of immersion
24. Use of achievement motivation
25. Use of personality selling exercises – the balloon debate
26. Use of finding opportunities (ideas for business)
27. Use of ways into business
28. Use of leveraging the student interest
29. Use of start-up frames, stages of start-up; tasks and learning needs
30. Use of the business plan as a relationship management instrument
31. Use of surviving in the early years of the venture
32. Use of segmenting the new venture programme market

33. Use of developing operations standards as a basis for estimating costs and controlling operations
34. Use of case studies
35. Use of exercises in finding ideas for business
36. Use of exploring the enterprise culture in a globalisation context
37. Use of programme evaluation
38. Use of the quiz
39. Use of undertaking an institutional audit
40. Use of sales pitch
41. Use of polls
42. Use of simulating entrepreneurial 'ways of'
43. Use of simulating the entrepreneurial 'life world'
44. Assessment

Further information with regards to the philosophical underpinnings that have led to the determination of the learning outcomes and recognition of the above noted teaching pedagogies can be found at the NCGE website, http://www.ncge.com.

References

Aldrich, Howard E. and Martha A. Martinez (2001), 'Many are called, but few are chosen: An evolutionary perspective for the study of entrepreneurship', *Entrepreneurship: Theory and Practice*, **25** (4), 41–57.

Aronsson, Magnus (2004), 'Education matters – but does entrepreneurship education?', *Academy of Management Learning & Education*, **3** (3), 289–92.

Banning, James H. (1978), *Campus Ecology: A Perspective for Student Affairs*, Cincinnati, OH: National Association of Student Personnel Administrators.

Baumol, William J. (1990), 'Entrepreneurship: Productive, unproductive, and destructive', *Journal of Political Economy*, **98** (5), 893–921.

Baxter-Magolda, Marcia (1998), 'Developing self-authorship in young adult life', *Journal of College Student Development*, **39** (2), 143–56.

Baxter-Magolda, Marcia (2004), *Making Their Own Way*, Virginia: Stylus.

Beard, Colin and John P. Wilson (2002), *Experiential Learning*, London: Kogan Page.

Bennett, Alexander L. and Andrew George (2003), *Case Studies and Theory Development in the Social Sciences*, Cambridge, MIT Press.

Bhaskar, Roy (1975), *A Realist Theory of Science*, Leeds, UK: Leeds Books.

Biggs, John (2003), *Teaching for Quality Learning at University: What the Student Does*, London: Open University Press.

Bjerke, Bjorn and Claes M. Hultman (2002), *Entrepreneurial Marketing: The Growth of Small Firms in the New Economic Era*, Cheltenham, UK and Northampton, MA, USA: Edward Elgar.

Blundel, Richard (2007), 'Critical realism: A suitable vehicle for entrepreneurship research', in Helle Neergaard and John P. Ulhøi (eds), *Handbook of Qualitative Research Methods in Entrepreneurship*, Cheltenham, UK and Northampton, MA, USA: Edward Elgar.

Boud, David, Rosemary Keogh and David Walker (1985), *Reflection: Turning Experience into Learning*, London: Routledge Falmer.

Brookfield, Stephen (1995), *Becoming a Critically Reflective Teacher*, San Francisco: Jossey-Bass.

Brown, Robert D. (1972), *Student Development in Tomorrow's Higher Education: A Return to the Academy*, Alexandria, VA: American College Personnel Association.

Bryk, Anthony S. and Barbara Schneider (2002), *Trust in Schools: A Core Resource for Improvement*, New York: Russell Sage Foundation.

Bygrave, William (2010), *Personal Communications*, 6th August 2010.

Choo, Stephen (2006), *Entrepreneurial Management*, Melbourne: Tilde University Press.

Clarke, George L. (1967), *Elements of Ecology*, New York: John Wiley & Sons.

Danermark, Berth, Mats Ekström, Liselotte Jakobsen and Jan Karlsson (2002), *Explaining Society: Critical Realism in the Social Sciences*, London: Routledge.

De Bono, Edward (1995), *Serious Creativity: Using the Power of Lateral Thinking to Create New Ideas*, London: HarperCollins Publishers.

DeGraff, Jeff and Katherine A. Lawrence (2002), *Creativity at Work*, San Francisco: John Wiley & Sons.

Dewey, John (1910), *How We Think,* Boston: D.C. Heath & Co.

Dewey, John (1922), *Human Nature and Conduct: An Introduction to Social Psychology*, New York: Henry Holt and Company.

English, Jack and Babette Moate (2009), *Discovering New Business Opportunities*, Sydney: Allen & Unwin.

European Commission (2008), *Entrepreneurship in Higher Education, Especially Within Non-Business Studies,* final report of the expert group, available at http://www.ec.europa.eu/enterprise.

Gartner, William B. (2001), 'Is there an elephant in entrepreneurship? Blind assumptions in theory development', *Entrepreneurship: Theory and Practice*, **25** (4), 27–40.

Gibb, Allan (2002), 'Creating conducive environments for learning and entrepreneurship: Living with, dealing with, creating and enjoying uncertainty and complexity', *Industry & Higher Education*, **16** (3), 135–48.

Gibb, Allan (2008), 'Entrepreneurship and enterprise education in schools and colleges: Insights from UK practice', *International Journal of Entrepreneurship Education*, **6**, 101–44.

Gibb, Allan (2010), *Compendium of Pedagogies for Teaching Entrepreneurship*, available at http://www.ncge.com.

Gould, Stephen J. (2002), *The Structure of Evolutionary Theory*, Cambridge, MA: Belknap Press of Harvard.

Gurin, Patricia (1999), 'New research on the benefits of diversity in college and beyond: An empirical analysis', *Diversity Digest*, **5**, available at http://www.diversityweb.org/Digest/Sp99/benefits.html.

Hart, Gail, Michael Clinton, Robyn Nash, Alan Barnard, Diane Collins, Deanne Gaskill, Marilyn Harris, Patsy Yates and Marion Mitchell (1998), *Stories from Experience: Monograph of Practice Incidents*, Brisbane: Queensland University of Technology.

Haskell, Edward F. (1949), 'A clarification of social science', *Main Currents in Modern Thought*, **7**, 45–51.

Hayward, Mathew L.A., W.R. Forster, S.D. Sarasvathy and B.L. Fredrickson (2009), 'Beyond hubris: How highly confident entrepreneurs rebound to venture again', *Journal of Business Venturing*, **25** (6), 569–78.

Healy, Marilyn and C. Perry (2000), 'Comprehensive criteria to judge validity and reliability of qualitative research within the realism paradigm', *Qualitative Market Research: An International Journal*, **3** (3), 118–26.

Heath, Roy (1964), *The Reasonable Adventurer*, Pittsburgh: University of Pittsburgh Press.

Hegarty, Cecilia and C. Jones (2008), 'Graduate entrepreneurship: More than child's play', *Education + Training*, **50** (7), 626–37.

Herrmann, K. (2008), *Developing Entrepreneurial Graduates – Putting Entrepreneurship at the Centre of Higher Education*, London: CIHE, NESTA, NCGE.

Hindle, Kevin (2007), 'Teaching entrepreneurship at university: From the wrong building to the right philosophy', in Patricia G. Greene and Mark P. Rice (eds), *Entrepreneurship Education*, Cheltenham, UK and Northampton, MA, USA: Edward Elgar.

Hinton, Geoffrey E. and S.J. Nowlan (1987), 'How learning can guide evolution', *Complex Systems*, **1**, 495–502.

Hodgson, Geoffrey M. (2001), 'Is social evolution Lamarckian or Darwinian?', in John Nightingale and John Laurent (eds), *Darwinism and Evolutionary Economics*, Cheltenham, UK and Northampton, MA, USA: Edward Elgar.

Hull, David (2001), *Science and Selection*, Cambridge, UK: Cambridge University Press.

Jones, Colin (2006a), 'Enterprise education: revisiting Whitehead to satisfy Gibbs', *Education + Training*, **48** (5), 336–47.

Jones, Colin (2006b), 'Guided by the philosophy of constructive alignment, directed by the realisation of niche construction', *Proceedings of the 29th HERDSA Conference: Critical Visions*, Perth, Australia, 10–13 July 2006.

Jones, Colin (2007), 'Creating the reasonable adventurer: The co-evolution of student and learning environment', *Journal of Small Business and Enterprise Development*, **14** (2), 228–40.

Jones, Colin (2009), 'Enterprise education: Learning through personal experience', *Journal of Industry and Higher Education*, **23** (3), 1–8.

Jones, Colin and J. English (2004), 'A contemporary approach to entrepreneurship education', *Education + Training*, **46** (8/9), 416–23.

Jones, Colin (2010a), 'Addressing the value dilemma of enterprise education: Rising to the ontological challenge', *Proceedings of the 7th AGSE International Entrepreneurship Exchange*, Sunshine Coast, Australia, 2–5 February 2010.

Jones, Colin (2010b), 'Accounting for student/educator diversity: Resurrecting Coaction theory', in A. Fayolle (ed), *Handbook of Research in Entrepreneurship Education, Vol. 3: International Perspectives*, Cheltenham, UK and Northampton, MA, USA: Edward Elgar.

Katz, Jerome A. (2003), 'The chronology and intellectual trajectory of American entrepreneurship education 1876–1999', *Journal of Business Venturing*, **18**, 283–300.

Keirsey, David and M. Bates (1984), *Please Understand Me: Character and Temperament Types*, Del Mar, CA: Gnosology Books.

Kim, Chan W. and R. Mauborgne (2000), 'Knowing a winning business idea when you see one', *Harvard Business Review*, **78** (5), 129–37.

King, Patricia M. and Karen S. Kitchener (1994), *Developing Reflective Judgment: Understanding and Promoting Intellectual Growth and Critical Thinking in Adolescents and Adults*, San Francisco: Jossey-Bass Publishers.

Kropotkin, Peter (1902), *Mutual Aid: A Factor of Evolution*, New York: McClure Phillips & Co.

Kuratko, Donald (2005), 'The emergence of entrepreneurship education: Development, trends, and challenges', *Entrepreneurship Theory and Practice*, **29** (5), 577–97.

Lange, Julian, A. Mollov, M. Pearlmutter, S. Singh and W.D. Bygrave (2007), 'Pre-startup formal business plans and post-startup performance: A study of 116 new ventures', *Venture Capital Journal*, **9** (4), 1–20.

Lansdell, Matthew (2009), *Towards a Model of Student Entrepreneurial Value*, unpublished Honours Dissertation, University of Tasmania.

Lewontin, Richard C. (1983), 'Gene, organism, and environment', in David S. Bendall (ed.), *Evolution from Molecules to Men*, Cambridge, UK: Cambridge University Press.

Lodish, Leonard, H.L. Morgan and A. Kallianpur (2001), *Entrepreneurial Marketing*, New York: John Wiley & Sons.

Magee, Bryan (1975), *Popper*, Glasgow: Fontana/Collins.

Mahoney, James (2003), 'Tentative answers to questions about causal mechanisms', *Proceedings of the American Political Science Association*, 28 August, Philadelphia, PA.

McWilliam, Erica L. (2009), 'Teaching for creativity: From sage to guide to meddler', *Asia Pacific Journal of Education*, **29** (3), 281–93.

Moltz, Barry (2003), *You Need to Be a Little Crazy: The Truth About Starting and Growing Your Business*, Chicago: Dearborn Trade Publishing.

Odling-Smee, John F. Kevin N. Laland and Marcus W. Feldman (2003), *Niche Construction: The Neglected Process in Evolution*, Oxford: Princeton University Press.

Palmer, Parker J. (1997), *The Courage to Teach: Exploring the Inner Landscape of a Teacher's Life*, San Francisco: Jossey-Bass.

Parker, Clyde A. (1978), *Encouraging Development in College Students*, Minneapolis, MN: University of Minnesota Press.

Peirce, Charles S. (1908), 'A neglected argument for the reality of god', *The Hibbert Journal*, **7** (1), 90–112.

Penaluna, Andrew J. Coates and K. Penaluna (2010), 'Creativity-based assessment and neural understandings: A discussion and case study analysis', *Education + Training*, **52** (8/9), 660–78.

Perry, William G. (1968), *Form of Intellectual and Ethical Development in the College Years: A Scheme*, New York: Holt, Rinehart & Winston.

Pianka, Eric R. (1973), 'The structure of lizard communities', *Annual Review of Ecology and Systematics*, **4**, 53–74.

Pittaway, Luke (2010), *Personal Communications*, 29th August 2010.

Scott, David (2001), *Realism and Educational Research: New Perspectives and Possibilities*, London: Routledge.

Sears, Paul B. (1980), *Deserts on the March*, Norman: University of Oklahoma Press.

Smilor, Raymond W. (1997), 'Entrepreneurship: Reflections on a subversive activity', *Journal of Business Venturing*, **12** (5), 341–46.

Stevenson, Howard H, Irving H. Grousbeck, Michael J. Roberts and Amar Bhide (1999), *New Business Ventures and the Entrepreneur*, (5th ed.), McGraw-Hill.

Storey, David (2009), *Personal Communications*, 14th July 2009.

Timmons, Jeffry A. (1999), *New Venture Creation: Entrepreneurship for the 21st Century*, San Francisco: Irwin McGraw-Hill.

Tyler, Ralph (1949), *Basic Principles of Curriculum and Instruction*, Chicago: The University of Chicago Press.

Veblen, Thorstein (1925), *The Theory of the Leisure Class*, London: George Allen & Unwin.

Volkmann, Christine (2009), *Educating the Next Wave of Entrepreneurs: Unlocking Entrepreneurial Capabilities to Meet the Global Challenges of the 21st Century*, Geneva: World Economic Forum.

Warwick Centre for Education and Industry (2001), *Independent Research into Learning for Enterprise and Entrepreneurship*, Warwick, UK: Warwick University.

Weber, Max (1968), *Economy and Society*, New York: Bedminster Press.
Whitehead, Alfred N. (1929), *The Aims of Education and Other Essays*, New York: The Free Press.

Index